SOUTHERN APPALACHIAN COUNTRY

BY GEORGE WUERTHNER

AMERICAN GEOGRAPHIC PUBLISHING

ROBERT C. SIMPSON

Left: *Vasey's trillium, a sign of spring.*
Far left: *Toccoa Falls, Georgia.*
Below: *The Louisiana water thrush favors forest interiors.*
Facing page, left: *Demonstrating quilting at the Dahlonega, Georgia "Gold Rush Days."*
Facing page, right: *On the Blue Ridge Parkway in Virginia.*

American Geographic Publishing is a corporation for publishing illustrated geographic information and guides. It is not associated with American Geographical Society. It has no commercial or legal relationship to and should not be confused with any other company, society or group using the words geographic or geographical in its name or its publications.

Library of Congress Cataloging-in-Publication Data

Wuerthner, George.
    Southern Appalachian country / by George Wuerthner.
        p.   cm.
    ISBN 0-938314-82-3
    1. Appalachian Region, Southern--Geography.   2. Natural history--Appalachian Region, Southern.   I. Title.
F217.A65W84   1990
917.5--dc20   90-38477

ROBERT C. SIMPSON

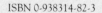

ISBN 0-938314-82-3

text © 1990 George Wuerthner
© 1990 American Geographic
    Publishing
P.O. Box 5630, Helena, MT 59604
(406) 443-2842

William A. Cordingley, Chairman
Rick Graetz, President & CEO
Mark O. Thompson, Director of
    Publications
Barbara Fifer, Production Manager
Design by Linda Collins
Printed in Hong Kong

TOM TILL

2

BELOW: AARON PASS; RIGHT: MARK E. GIBSON

ABOUT THE AUTHOR

George Wuerthner is the author of eight other books, including seven from American Geographic Publishing. He also is an outdoor photographer who works with a 4x5 view camera. His photography has appeared in hundreds of publications, including *Outside, Arizona Highways*, and *Wilderness* magazines, and Sierra Club and National Geographic Society books, as well as in museum exhibits here and abroad. A former botanist, biologist, university instructor and wilderness ranger, Wuerthner has traveled widely throughout North America. While not on the road, he resides in Livingston, Montana just north of Yellowstone National Park.

He thanks David Wheeler of *Katúah Journal* for suggestions on this manuscript.

AUDREY GIBSON

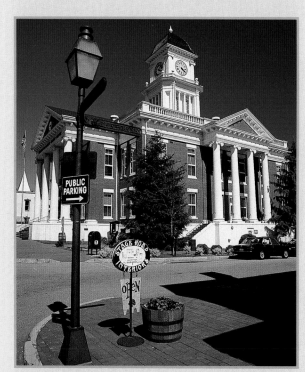

KEN LAYMAN/PHOTO AGORA

4

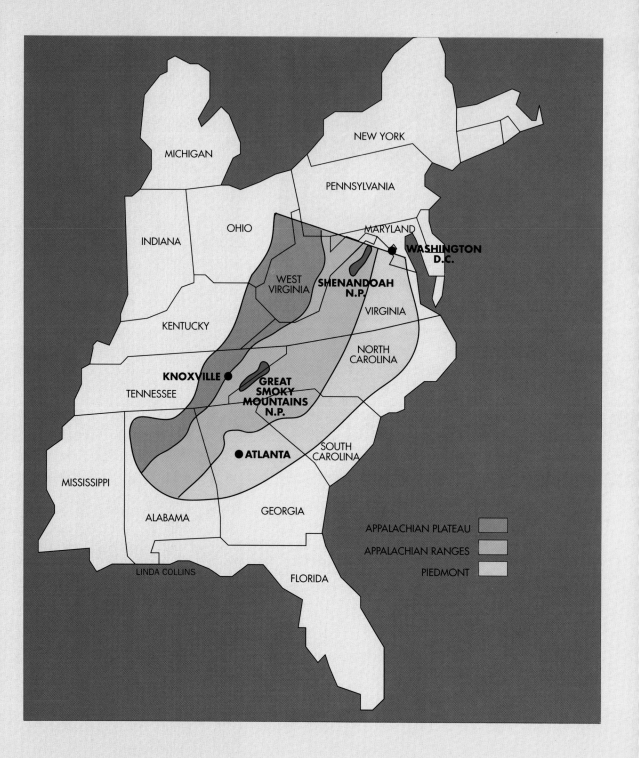

MICHIGAN

NEW YORK

PENNSYLVANIA

OHIO

MARYLAND

INDIANA

WASHINGTON D.C.

WEST VIRGINIA

SHENANDOAH N.P.

VIRGINIA

KENTUCKY

NORTH CAROLINA

KNOXVILLE ●

GREAT SMOKY MOUNTAINS N.P.

TENNESSEE

●ATLANTA

SOUTH CAROLINA

MISSISSIPPI

ALABAMA

GEORGIA

APPALACHIAN PLATEAU

APPALACHIAN RANGES

LINDA COLLINS

PIEDMONT

FLORIDA

CONTENTS

*Front cover: Sunrise in Pisgah National Forest, North Carolina, seen
from the Blue Ridge Parkway.* GEORGE WUERTHNER
Back cover, top left: Periwinkle. SCOTT T. SMITH
Top right: Near Volney, Virginia. GEORGE WUERTHNER
Bottom: Chickamauga National Military Park, Georgia.
GEORGE WUERTHNER

*Title page: Noland Divide and Thomas Ridge from Clingmans
Dome.* LARRY ULRICH

Left: Shot Beech Ridge and Deep Creek Valley in the Great Smokies.
Facing page, top: Boiling peanuts in North Carolina.
*Facing page, bottom: Washington County Courthouse, Jones-
borough, Tennessee.*

LARRY ULRICH   **5**

1

INTRODUCTION

Mention the Southern Appalachian Mountains and different images come to different folks. Some think of blue, mist-covered ridges, of the Great Smoky Mountains piled one after another to the far horizon. Others recall mountain people with their cabins, crafts and self-sufficiency, or miners working in underground coal fields. Still others conjure up thoughts of waterfalls in hardwood coves or brook trout gliding across limpid pools.

Each of these images is correct. There is no single description that completely covers the diversity of the Southern Appalachian region.

Perhaps because of this, there is no consensus on what exactly constitutes the Southern Appalachian Mountains. The Appalachian Mountain chain, the second-largest mountain system in North America after the Rockies, stretches all the way from northern Georgia to Newfoundland in Canada. Just what part of this 2,000-mile-long mountain uplands constitutes the Southern Appalachians is less definite.

Like the Rocky Mountains of the West, the Appalachians are broken into many subdivisions with individual local names—Longfellow Mountains in Maine, White Mountains in New Hampshire, Green Mountains in Vermont, Allegheny Mountains of West Virginia and Pennsylvania, and Great Smoky Mountains on the North Carolina-Tennessee border. Yet, for all the different names, it is often difficult to discern just where one range ends and another begins.

Nearly everyone agrees that the Southern Appalachians begin in northern Georgia and lie west of the piedmont foothills of western North Carolina and southwestern Virginia. However, defining the mountains' northern and western edges becomes a little less certain.

Most geologists define the Southern Appalachians as the belt of metamorphic rock we call the Blue Ridge Mountains lying south of the Roanoke River. Metamorphic rocks are either sedimentary or volcanic rocks changed by heat and pressure into a new kind of rock—for example, marble is metamorphosed limestone.

Geographers, on the other hand, have an expanded view that places the northern limits of the Southern Appalachians near Carlisle, Pennsylvania. They refer to this entire region as the Blue Ridge Mountains Physiographic province. If you travel the Skyline Drive in Shenandoah National Park or the Blue Ridge Parkway, or visit Great Smoky Mountains National Park, you are within the Blue Ridge Physiographic province.

However, not everyone is satisfied with limiting the Southern Appalachians to the Blue Ridge alone. West of the Blue Ridge lies the Great Valley—a structural trough that runs from the Hudson Valley in New York south into Alabama. The Cumberland Valley of Pennsylvania and Maryland, Shenandoah Valley of Virginia, and the Tennessee River Valley of East Tennessee all are names for this same valley system. Beyond the Great Valley are more uplands that include the Appalachian Plateau, and Valley and Ridge provinces west of the main Blue Ridge Crest in West Virginia, Kentucky and eastern Tennessee. The highlands of the Appalachian Plateau country include both the Cumberland and Allegheny mountains.

The rocks that make up both the Valley and Ridge and the Appalachian Plateau are essentially the same. But the difference in topography is the result of their geological his-

LARRY ULRICH

Above: Autumn along the Catawba River as seen from the Blue Ridge Parkway, North Carolina.

Facing page: Morning mist on Lake Chatuge, Georgia, at the southern limits of the Southern Appalachians.

8

tory. The Valley and Ridge portion of the Appalachians consists of folded sedimentary rocks, while in the plateaus farther west, the same rocks retain their original horizontal positions, the reason for their flat-topped but stream-dissected uplands. Both of these regions consist of rocks younger than found those in the metamorphic zone of the Blue Ridge.

So what do I consider the Southern Appalachians? For the purposes of this book, I will take the more conservative view and define the Southern Appalachians as the mountainous region lying south of the Roanoke River and north of Springer Mountain, Georgia. The Tennessee Valley bounds it on the west and separates it from the plateaus still farther west. Although the focus of the book will be this area, where appropriate to the larger understanding of the Southern Appalachians region, I will occasionally include relevant information the Valley and Ridge, and Appalachian Plateau, or what may be called the coal-bearing region of this southern highlands.

Even though this area is smaller than some might define as the Southern Appalachians, it still is a rather extensive uplands, equal in size to all of New England and New York state combined. This sprawling area is a high, sparsely settled country with scattered small settlements and towns, and even fewer cities. Asheville, North Carolina is the only sizable community entirely within the region. Many areas with large public land holdings are almost unpopulated. On the Tennessee border, Swain County in North Carolina has a population density of only 21 people per square mile. Several other counties in western North Carolina have fewer than 28 people per square mile—the average for Colorado, a wide-open western state. Although not reaching the high elevations of Colorado's lofty mountains, the Southern Appalachians do present a substantial uplands if measured from base to summit. For instance, 6,593-foot Mount LeConte in Great Smoky Mountains National Park on the Tennessee-North Carolina border rises more than a mile above the city of Gatlinburg, which lies at 1,250 feet.

While only one summit north of the Potomac reaches above 6,000 feet (Mt. Washington in New Hampshire), in the Southern Appalachians 46 peaks reach this height or greater. Within the Smokies alone, 16 mountain summits top out at or above 6,000 feet.

Not surprisingly, the highest point in each of the southeastern states is found within the Southern Appalachians region, including Virginia's 5,729-foot Mt. Rogers, North Carolina's 6,684-foot Mt. Mitchell, Georgia's 4,784-foot Brasstown Bald, South Carolina's 3,560-foot Sassafras Mountain and Tennessee's 6,643-foot Clingmans Dome. High points in the Appalachian Plateau country to the west include West Virginia's highest point, 4,863-foot Spruce Knob, and Kentucky's 4,145-foot Black Mountain.

As a general rule the Southern Appalachians are lower in the north than in the south. Their width also varies from north to south. In its northern reaches, the Blue Ridge is just that—a ridge. In most of Shenandoah National Park, for example, it is seldom more than five miles wide. However, once you travel south of the Roanoke River, the Southern Appalachians broaden and reach their greatest width in North Carolina. In places, the mountains and their foothills are more than 150 miles across.

In western North Carolina and eastern Tennessee, the Blue Ridge province is actually two parallel ridges. The eastern branch retains the name Blue Ridge and extends south into South Carolina and Georgia while the western prong—known under the collective name of Unaka Mountains—lies along the Tennessee-North Carolina border. The Great Smokies are part of the highest portion of the Unakas. These two great arms reunite in northern Georgia, coming together at Springer Mountain, the southern terminus of the Appalachian Trail.

Smaller individual ridges and peak complexes such as Roan Mountain, Bald Mountains, Nantahala Mountains, Unicoi Mountains, Cowee Mountains, Balsam Mountains, and the Cheoah Mountains form part of the main divides and cross rungs between them. Mt. Mitchell, highest point in the eastern United States at 6,684 feet, lies in yet another cross range—the Black Range.

Despite their overall height, the Southern Appalachians were too far south to support glaciers during the last Ice

JEFF GNASS

JIM HAMILTON

Above: *In the Shenandoah Valley of Virginia, a part of the Great Valley system that stretches from the Hudson River to northern Alabama.*
Left: *Gatlinburg, Tennessee, developed for tourists at the western entrance of Great Smoky Mountains National Park.*

Facing page: *Snow covers red spruce on Clingmans Dome in the Great Smoky Mountains on the Tennessee-North Carolina border. The Smokies are among the highest mountains in the eastern United States, with 16 summits that rise above 6,000 feet.*

9

Above: *Mossy tree trunk is an indication of the abundant precipitation that gives the Southern Appalachians the distinction of having the second-greatest annual average precipitation in the U.S. after the Pacific Northwest. Seen here, along the Little River in Great Smoky Mountains National Park.*

Facing page: *Horizontal bedding of sedimentary rock strata is visible in Cloudland Canyon, Cloudland Canyon State Park, Georgia.*

The abundance of plant and animal life is partially a reflection of a generally mild climate and abundant rainfall. While the highest peaks occasionally have temperatures low enough to make even a New Englander shiver—a temperature of 34 below zero once was recorded on North Carolina's Mt. Mitchell—below-freezing temperatures are of short duration and relatively rare, especially on the lower slopes and valleys. In fact, continuous snow cover is relatively rare except for the highest elevations—and then only for short periods each winter. Summer temperatures, particularly in the lowland valleys, are often in the 90s and accompanied by high humidity. However, the highest mountain reaches are usually cooler. The lodge on top of Mt. LeConte in the Great Smokies has never recorded a temperature above 80 degrees and Mt. Mitchell has only been only slightly warmer at 81 degrees.

Nevertheless, the luxuriant plant growth in the Southern Appalachians is partially the result of abundant, year-round precipitation. The Southern Appalachians receives the second-highest average rainfall in the entire country outside the Pacific Northwest. Highlands, in the southern mountains of North Carolina, has recorded more than 100 inches of precipitation in a single year. During the summer months in Great Smoky Mountains National Park, rainfall in excess of an inch a day occurs at least 10 days a month. Annual precipitation falls off as one moves north and west from the North Carolina-Georgia border. For instance, much of the George Washington National Forest in Virginia receives approximately 30 to 35 inches annually.

When the first Europeans began to explore these rich forestlands, the Southern Appalachians were home to the Cherokee Indians. The Cherokee hunted the slopes and carved small fields from the forested river valleys to grow corn and other crops.

As the coastal areas of the East Coast began to fill up, venturesome pioneers cut rough roads through the forests, first passing through the Appalachians and later settling in them. But, for the most part, people flowed around these mountains, and after the initial settlement, the Southern Appalachians were largely ignored by the main events of

Age. As a consequence these geologically old, rolling uplands have been a refugium for many plant and animal species. In fact, this region is one of two centers for biological diversity in North America, supporting more than half the species of trees, flowering plants and ferns found in North America. Better than 100 species of trees are reported for Great Smoky Mountains National Park alone—more than are found in all of northern Europe. More than 2,000 species of fungi and mushrooms are reported for the relatively small area protected within Great Smoky Mountains National Park and well beyond 400 species of mosses live in the Southern Appalachians, nearly one third of all species known in North America.

11

history. In the isolation of the hollows and narrow valleys, small farms and settlements, the people of the Southern Appalachian region retained many vestiges of early American culture. Preserved in the mountain coves were dialects spiced with many Scotch-Irish words of the early settlers, along with traditional subsistence lifestyles and skills.

Around the turn of the 20th century, the mountains were invaded by logging companies. Nearly all accessible lands were stripped of trees. Besides providing jobs for local mountaineers, the railroad tracks built by the logging companies ended the isolation that had dominated the region for so long.

The wreckage and ruin resulting in denuded hillsides and eroded slopes prompted an outcry across the country by those who wanted to buy the timber company holdings and allow the land to reforest. Unlike the national parks and forests in the western United States, largely created from existing federal lands, the Eastern national forests and parks all had to be purchased from private holdings. Today six national forests—the Jefferson, Nantahala, Pisgah, Chattahoochee, Cherokee and part of the Sumter—plus the Great Smoky Mountains National Park and the Blue Ridge Parkway collectively total 3.5 million acres of federal holdings in the Southern Appalachian region. In addition, the nearby federal lands beyond the Southern Appalachian region, including the Monangahela National Forest in West Virginia and George Washington National Forest in Virginia along with Shenandoah National Park—add another 2 million acres to the total federal holdings in the region. Nearly all these lands were purchased from private owners, frequently timber companies. They were largely lands already cut over, and as a result there is very little virgin, old-growth forest in the Southern Appalachians.

The federally acquired mountain lands in the Southern Appalachians now provide the foundation for the long-impoverished region's growing tourist industry—generating wealth as well as environmental problems.

In 1988, tourists spent $839,604,000 in the 19-county area that makes up western North Carolina. By the year 2000, tourism and travel is expected to be the dominant industry for the entire Southern Appalachian region. This is not surprising considering that this upland region is within a day's drive of nearly half the U.S. population. More than 10 million people visited Great Smoky Mountains National Park in 1987, and the Pisgah and Nantahala national forests in North Carolina together are visited by more than 24 million people annually, more than the combined visitation of the top 10 national parks! Anyone who has seen the growth of Pigeon Forge or Gatlinburg, Tennessee in recent years will not doubt that tourism has become a major industry of the region.

In addition to the influx of tourists, retirees and others are moving to the mountains for the quality of life. Many areas of the Southern Appalachians are outpacing the nation in population growth. For instance, the 19 counties that make up western North Carolina have grown 25 percent in population since 1970, going from 551,793 to 691,140, and they are still growing. Nantahala Power and Light—which serves Highlands, North Carolina, long known as a desirable second-home area—reported a 31 percent increase in growth rate since 1981. Other communities, like Hendersonville and Brevard, have experienced extravagant growth, due chiefly to an influx of retirees.

While this growth has been an economic boost for an area long known for its poverty, the unbridled development threatens the very qualities drawing people to the region. With little planning or zoning, small towns can quickly become clogged with traffic. New roads bulldozed up steep mountainsides cause sedimentation, which threatens water quality and fisheries. Leaky or improperly located septic systems allow untreated sewage to move into streams and groundwater. And smog is increasingly becoming a problem: air pollutants are easily trapped in mountain basins, and cities like Asheville sometimes are blanketed with a dense haze.

But not all the problem is local. The blue haze that gave the Great Smokies its name was mostly a result of high humidity mixed with natural compounds. Today that haze is largely a mixture of acid sulfates produced by coal-fired power plants and other industrial sources in the Ohio

and Tennessee valleys, along with emissions from automobiles. Now, during the summer in Great Smokies National Park, there are visibility problems on 85 percent of the days. Atmospheric deposition and acid rainfall from factories and power plants to the west are increasingly thought to be major factors in the decline of red spruce on mountain tops, and a contributing factor in the death of flowering dogwood trees throughout the Southern Appalachians.

The problem of air pollution demonstrates that no region is entirely isolated from the problems affecting other areas. There is a tremendous need for a regional approach in planning as well as greater cooperation between various local, state and federal agencies if the biological integrity of the Southern Appalachians is to survive.

Above: *The Blue Ridge province broadens into a belt of mountains more than a hundred miles wide in North Carolina, creating a sea of peaks—as seen here from near Cold Mountain, Pisgah National Forest, North Carolina.*

Facing page: *The great abundance of flowering shrubs and trees is one of the distinctive features of the Southern Appalachians. Here, flowering dogwood along Big Creek, Great Smoky Mountains National Park.*

APPALACHIAN TRAIL

Right: Hikers on the Appalachian Trail, the 2,000-mile-long footpath along the spine of the Appalachian chain from Georgia all the way to Maine.

Facing page: View from Albert Mountain on the Appalachian Trail, south toward the Southern Nantahala Wilderness on the North Carolina-Georgia border

Hikers in the Southern Appalachians are bound to come across white, two-by-six-inch rectangular trail markers painted on trees and rocks. The symbol marks the Appalachian Trail, a 2,100-mile footpath that traverses the backbone of the range from Maine to Georgia. It's the longest footpath in the world and passes through 14 states en route. The highest point on the entire trail is Clingmans Dome in Great Smoky Mountains National Park.

The trail begins on Springer Mountain in northern Georgia. From there the trail winds northwest, generally following the crest of the Blue Ridge into North Carolina, where it swings west to the Tennessee-North Carolina border. By the time it reaches Virginia, it's once again on the spine of the Blue Ridge, often side by side with the Blue Ridge Parkway and Skyline Drive in Shenandoah National Park. The Appalachian Trail crosses the Potomac River at Harper's Ferry and continues all the way to Maine.

The idea to construct a trail traversing much of the Appalachian Mountains can be attributed to one person, U.S. Forest Service planner Benton MacKaye of Shirley Center, Massachusetts. In 1921, MacKaye published an article in the *Journal of the American Institute of Architects* entitled: "The Appalachian Trail: A Project in Regional Planning," which outlined the concept of a through route to connect many diverse portions of the Appalachian Range. The idea caught on.

As originally conceived by MacKaye, the trail would link New Hampshire's Mt. Washington, the highest peak in the Northern Appalachians, with Mt. Mitchell in North Carolina, the highest peak in the Southern Appalachians. People debated the trail concept, and chose to extend the southern terminus to Lookout Mountain near Chattanooga, and to Mt. Katahdin in Maine at the northern end. Georgia's Mt. Oglethorpe later was chosen over Lookout Mountain as the southern terminus. In 1958 the southern terminus was rerouted to Springer Mountain, because of development at Mt. Oglethorpe.

Some sections of the trail were already in existence, such as the Long Trail in Vermont's Green Mountains. But the majority of the pathway had to be scouted and built by volunteers between 1921 and 1937. Hiking clubs sprang up along the route and each took charge of securing its section of the trail. Today more than 65 different clubs, along with the National Park Service and National Forest Service, maintain the trail, access trails and lean-tos.

In 1968 the Appalachian Trail was designated a National Scenic Trail by Congress and in 1978 Congress passed the Appalachian Trail Bill authorizing the purchase of lands on either side of the trail corridor by the federal government. The Appalachian Trail Conference Trust also helps to buy land. In addition, since the trail was routed to pass through lands in public ownership, much of the route already is protected within eight national forests (including six in the southern Appalachians) and six National Park Service areas. In an average year, some 100 hikers walk the entire length of the trail, and each year approximately 4 million people trace some portion of it. As a recreational asset, the trail has been a huge success.

GEORGE WUERTHNER PHOTOS BOTH PAGES

In recent years, support has grown to preserve both wilderness and biological diversity along the Appalachian Trail. In the footsteps of MacKaye several visionary proposals would link wilderness and roadless areas along the trail into a wildlands corridor running the entire length of the Appalachian Range. Perhaps one of the most persuasive advocates is Jamie Sayen, of Preserve Appalachian Wilderness, who has promoted the concept of wilderness restoration for undeveloped portions of the entire Appalachian Range. Sayen believes the Appalachian Trail corridor should be recognized as an important and perhaps critical pathway for the movement and preservation of plant and animal species. If protected, the corridor could go a long way towards reducing the potential deleterious effects of genetic isolation and inbreeding resulting from habitat fragmentation. As Sayens envisions it, the Appalachian Trail would serve as the link between existing designated wilderness areas and "wilderness recovery areas" to be allowed over time to revert to a more natural state.

15

2

GEOLOGY

THE OLDEST MOUNTAINS

The Appalachian Mountains are among the oldest mountains in North America. Their rounded shapes are one expression of this great age. Known as a fold-and-thrust mountain system, the Appalachians are formed of rocks once part of a huge ocean basin where sediments collected to tremendous depths. Subsequent geological events gave rise to the three major geological provinces we recognize in the greater Southern Appalachians today—Blue Ridge; Valley and Ridge; and Appalachian Plateau. Each owes its different appearance to its geological history.

The mountains of the Blue Ridge physiographic province are largely metamorphic and igneous rocks. Metamorphic rocks are sedimentary rocks changed by heat and pressure. In the Blue Ridge province, they include gneisses, schists and quartzites. The igneous rocks, formed from molten rock deep in the earth, include granites.

These rocks are often called basement rocks since they may make up the core rocks on most continents. If you could dig deep enough almost everywhere on the North American continent, you would find these basement rocks. They usually are covered by younger rocks and sediments, so one seldom sees them except in mountainous areas where uplift and erosion have stripped away the overlying rocks.

Metamorphic or igneous, all are erosion-resistant rocks, and so remain as the highest ridges and summits of this province, including the Great Smoky Mountains,

Unakas, Black Mountains and the Blue Ridge itself. Since these rocks no longer have any sedimentary layering, or were originally molten rock deep in the earth, it is not surprising that there are no fossils to be found among the rocks of the Blue Ridge.

VALLEY AND RIDGE PROVINCE

To the west of the Blue Ridge lies the Valley and Ridge province. The Valley and Ridge is a region of folded sedimentary rocks bent into broad anticlines and synclines, or waves of rock.

The original horizontal layering of sediments has been crumpled into folds, thus is no longer in the position originally laid down. Huge slices of sedimentary rock have been pushed westward and ride up and over other strata, much like cards in a deck being shuffled.

However, if you go far enough west to the Appalachian Plateau, these same sedimentary rock strata, identical to the rock layers in the Valley and Ridge province, also are found. They are exactly the same except they are still horizontal. They form plateaus dissected by deep river gorges like the New and Russell Fork. Nevertheless, until the strata of the Valley and Ridge province were folded, the geologic histories of both regions were identical.

The sediments that make up both the Valley and Ridge and Appalachian plateaus were laid down in shallow seas. Originally, sands washed into the ocean from a continent that lay to the east. Gradually, a tropical sea washed over these sandy deposits. Limestones and dolomites—formed only in warm waters—covered the sands.

These changes in sediment deposition mark changes in plates that make up the earth's surface. The Appalachian Mountains are the result of a continual shifting, colliding and ripping apart of huge crustal plates, according to the theory of plate tectonics. As these continent-sized plates

Above: *Water-polished boulders along the Middle Prong of the Little Pigeon River.*

Facing page: *The parallel ridges of the Valley and Ridge province are evident in this view from Powell Mountain, southwest Virginia.*

16

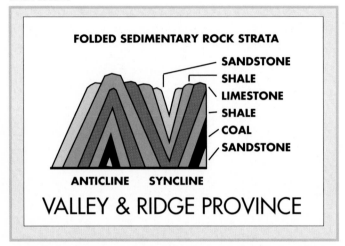

FOLDED SEDIMENTARY ROCK STRATA

SANDSTONE
SHALE
LIMESTONE
SHALE
COAL
SANDSTONE

ANTICLINE   SYNCLINE

VALLEY & RIDGE PROVINCE

move about the surface of the earth, floating on a molten layer of magma, they have created and destroyed mountain ranges. Right now the North American continental plate is drifting westward, with the Atlantic Ocean opening up ever wider in its wake.

The Southern Appalachians owe their existence to three major mountain-building events associated with the past movement of these crustal plates. About 450 million years ago, sometime after the sedimentary rocks that make up Valley and Ridge and Appalachian plateaus were laid down, the Taconic Orogeny began to push up highlands along the edge of the continent.

COLLISIONS OF PLATES

This mountain-building epoch resulted when the land mass that would be North America collided with a number of small continents or large islands. The force of the collision crumpled the earth's crust along the contact between these two plates like the front of a car that has run into a wall. The sedimentary rocks were altered by heat into metamorphic rocks. The farther east you move in the Appalachians—toward the original region of collision along the old plate boundaries—the more deformed and meta-

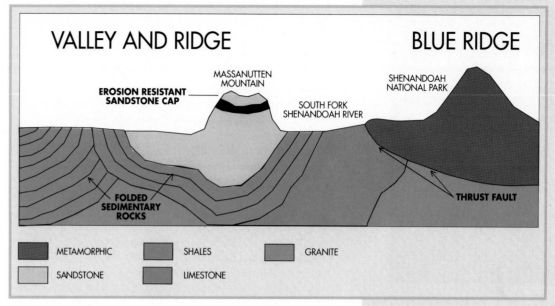

VALLEY AND RIDGE   **BLUE RIDGE**

MASSANUTTEN MOUNTAIN

EROSION RESISTANT SANDSTONE CAP

SHENANDOAH NATIONAL PARK

SOUTH FORK SHENANDOAH RIVER

FOLDED SEDIMENTARY ROCKS

THRUST FAULT

METAMORPHIC   SHALES   GRANITE

SANDSTONE   LIMESTONE

morphosed the rocks become. Bodies of granite tend to be formed along the margins of colliding plates, and in the Southern Appalachians granite is most abundant along the eastern edge of the Blue Ridge province, which was closest to the old plate border.

Not only did mountains develop, but also island pieces were cemented onto the North American continent. Since they originated elsewhere, the rocks of these island pieces seem out of place—they don't match nearby rocks. Geologists call these pieces of crust "suspect terranes."

Meanwhile, sediments eroded from the mountains continued to pile up in the adjoining sea that lay to the west. Some of these would later become the extremely erosion-resistant sandstones that cap Clinch Mountain in southwest Virginia and Massanutten Mountain in the Shenandoah Valley.

Another collision between islands and the North American crustal plate occurred some 100 million years later. Known as the Acadian orogeny, this collision caused further metamorphism of rocks along the continental margin. Erosion off the highlands dumped more sediments in shallow seas and swamps. As plants and animals died, many areas were buried by sediments before they had completely decayed. These layers of undecayed organic material, under the influence of heat and pressure and with a liberal dose of time, were transformed into the coal now so pervasive throughout the Appalachian Plateau country west of the Blue Ridge.

Then, about 300 to 250 million years ago, what is now North America joined Greenland and Europe to form a super-continent called Laurussia. This super-continent straddled the equator and its climate was warm and humid.

The initial rise of the Southern Appalachians was the result of collision over a 50-million-year period between two super-continents: Laurussia, upon which the Southern Appalachians rode, and Gondwana made up of Africa, South America and India. What we know now as the Southern Appalachians slowly began to buckle and rise. By 290 million years ago, all the continents were united into a giant super-continent known as Pangaea.

The collision and subsequent joining of Laurussia and Gondwana formed an overthrust belt 1,100 miles long. Older rock strata were pushed up and over younger ones, trending from southeast to northwest. The Blue Ridge in Shenandoah National Park, for example, rests on top of rock of the Shenandoah Valley that lies to the west. This belt of overthrust older rock lying on top of younger rock is particularly wide in North Carolina, where rocks have been pushed dozens of miles westward.

Organic sediments trapped in the rock formed oil and gas deposits that interest the oil industry today. A similar overthrust belt exists in the western United States and Canada as well, and the oil fields of Alberta, Wyoming, and western Colorado are parts of this large zone.

GEOLOGICAL WINDOWS

In a number of areas, the older rock of this overthrust belt has completely eroded away, exposing the younger rocks beneath in what geologists call a "window." Several famous windows exist, including the Grandfather Mountain Window along the Blue Ridge Parkway. Linville Falls tumbles over a ledge of old metamorphic gneiss and into a pool formed in rock nearly a half billion years younger.

Above: Metamorphic rocks of the Blue Ridge province have been pushed westward by a thrust fault over the younger sedimentary rocks of the Valley and Ridge province. If you dug deep enough, you would reach basement rock, in most cases granite.

Facing page, left: Contorted metamorphic rock of the Blue Ridge province, seen at Black Balsam Knob, Pisgah National Forest, North Carolina.
Right: Originally horizontal layers of sediment, the rock of the Valley and Ridge province has been crumpled and folded.

19

Above: *The "Cockcomb," an erosion-resistant rock layer, caps North Mountain, Virginia.*
Top: *Throughout the Valley and Ridge province, sandstones form hard, erosion-resistant caps, thus remain as uplands and ridges like this one that forms Lookout Mountain on the Tennessee-Georgia border.*

Cades Cove is another well known geological window found on the Tennessee side of Great Smoky Mountain National Park. Cades Cove is a valley completely surrounded by mountains—whose rocks are actually older than the rocks in the valley below. The rocks exposed on the valley floor are limestones, which eroded into rich, fertile soils that once supported productive farming.

The Laurussia-Gondwana collision also folded the sedimentary rock strata of sandstone, shale and limestone—originally laid down in ancient seas west of the Blue Ridge—into what is now known as the Valley and Ridge province. The rocks of the Valley and Ridge are no different than those that make up the Appalachian Plateaus farther west in West Virginia, Kentucky and Tennessee. The only difference is that the Valley and Ridge province was closer to the area of collision, hence they were crumpled more.

SCULPTED BY EROSION

Some of these crumpled, folded sedimentary layers were more easily eroded than others. Rocks such as limestone became the valleys, while harder layers such as sandstone remained as ridges—for instance Massanutten Mountain, Powell Mountain and other major uplands of the Valley and Ridge province. The Great Valley, which includes Shenandoah, and the Valley of East Tennessee are both areas where limestones and other easily erodable sedimentary rocks dominate.

Since caverns are formed in limestone or limestone derivatives like dolomite or marble, most of the region's caverns are found in the Valley and Ridge province. Naturally occurring acids in water percolated through and gradually dissolved the rock, leaving caverns. There are thousands of caverns along the length of the Great Valley limestone belt, with 2,500 in Virginia alone.

The limestones of the Shenandoah Valley and elsewhere formed under tropical seas, yet the creation of Pangaea uplifted them to form dry land. Subsequent continental collision drove the Appalachians to even greater heights and blocked the movement of air masses. The lands west of the mountains changed from swamps to deserts. The drying landscape forced some animals to adapt to a land existence. Evolution favored those animals that laid eggs with hard shells. They could survive on land, far from water, and had a competitive advantage over amphibians that relied upon water for part of their life cycles. We know the egg-layers today as reptiles. Eventually the reptiles diversified, and included large animals we call dinosaurs.

The union of the super-continents had other implications for evolution. Similar species that once resided on different land masses were thrown together and competition was keen. Many animals and plants disappeared during this period, the time of one of the most intense periods of extinctions known on earth.

Then, around 205 million years ago, Pangaea began to break apart. North America split away from Africa about where present-day Morocco is located, and the Atlantic Ocean was born. Parts of old continental plates were torn loose and welded onto the new ones—Boston, for example, rests upon crust that once may have been part of Africa. North America is still moving away from Europe at a rate of two to three inches a year.

Many plant and animal species found in the Southern Appalachians are similar to those in other, widely divergent parts of the earth. For instance, forests with species composition very similar to those in the Southern Appalachians are found in China. Once, all these widely dispersed forests had a common continental heritage. However, as the continents separated, animals and plants then evolved in isolation.

All the time the Appalachians have been rising, erosion, primarily from water, has been tearing them down. Once, they probably were as rugged as the Rockies or the Sierras, but time has softened the edges and rounded the contours. The softer rocks were more easily eroded than harder ones and consequently what we see today as peaks and ridges are mostly harder rock strata, while the valleys and coves are softer strata.

Today the Appalachians lie on the trailing, not advancing, end of a continental mass. As a consequence,

(continued on page 22)

COAL

The Carboniferous period was named for the large deposits of coal (or carbon) that formed around 300 million years ago. Coal seams are abundant in the Valley and Ridge or Appalachian provinces of southwestern Virginia, eastern Kentucky and West Virginia. However, coal is not known among the metamorphic and igneous rocks of the Blue Ridge Physiological province.

Coal occurs in strata along with other sedimentary rocks, usually shales and sandstones. Coal is nothing more than poorly decomposed plant material with a minimum of inorganic matter, which accumulated in ancient lowlands with poor drainage. Swampy conditions with stagnant, oxygen-poor water that limits biological decomposition are prerequisites for the formation of coal. As partially decomposed plant material collects, it is buried by new sediments. This early stage of coal development we call peat. As more sediments are laid down on top, heat and pressure over millions of years change the peat further. First, it becomes lignite, then subbituminous coal and finally bituminous coal—at which point the original peat deposit has been compressed to one tenth its original thickness. At each stage in the change from peat to bituminous coal, the proportion of carbon increases, as well as the amount of heat the coal will produce.

If the coal seams are folded, the pressure and heat will change bituminous coal into anthracite, which is a metamorphic rock. Anthracite has even more carbon than bituminous coal, hence burns even hotter and cleaner.

Coal formation is occurring today along the eastern seaboard. Dismal Swamp in Virginia, for example, has peat deposits six feet thick. Given a generous dose of millions of years, the peat of the Dismal Swamp may end up as coal.

There are several methods for mining coal. Where seams are near the surface *(above)*, the overburden is stripped away and the coal dug with giant shovels. In other instances *(left)*, giant augers are used to drill out the coal seams.

21

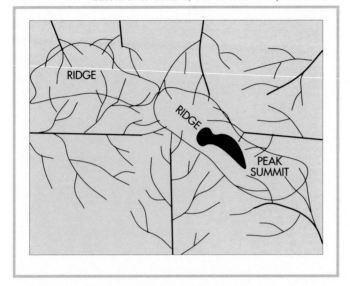

there is not much geological activity compared to currently active plate margins such as the coast of California, where frequent earthquakes are indications of plate collisions we can't see.

The legacy of geological history is readily visible to a knowing eye. Faults are broken or cracked pieces of the crust. They often define where valleys will occur or mountains will rise. The mile-high rise of Mt. LeConte above Gatlinburg, for example, is marked by the Greenbrier Fault, and the nearly linear valley of the Oconaluftee River in Great Smoky Mountains National Park follows the structural weakness created by the Oconaluftee Fault.

Since streams erode soft rock most easily, the pattern of water courses is dictated by the region's geology. For instance, in the Valley and Ridge province, the long linear valleys interrupted by high ridges create a notable branching pattern with long parallel main branches interrupted by short feeder tributaries. On the other hand, the more or less evenly mixed metamorphic rocks of the Blue Ridge make no particular patterns and stream drainages are dendritic, or like the veins of a leaf.

The Southern Appalachians were too far south to support Ice Age glaciers, and so they hold no glacial landforms like cirques, finger lakes and moraines common in the northern reaches of the Appalachian Mountains in New England. However, the cooler temperatures during the past glacial period did increase the amount of frost cracking or ice-wedging. Water trapped in cracks freezes and expands. Repeated over and over, such ice can split boulders. If ice-wedging fractures the rock on cliffs, debris accumulates at the bases to form a jumble of rocks and boulders called a talus slope.

It's interesting to consider that the current scenic landscape and land-use patterns often reflect a collection of random geologic events which may span a billion or more years. Our roads follow valleys dictated by faults, crossing mountain range through water gaps carved by rivers. Our most productive farms lie upon the soils derived from rocks that once were ancient seas, while the coal used to power our lights and appliances was once a swampy forest. The dramatic scenery that draws visitors to places like the Great Smoky Mountains is the aftermath of continental collisions millions of years ago. Next time you stop to admire the view from some overlook, spend a moment contemplating the ancient and dynamic geological past that makes the Southern Appalachians what it is today.

Left: *Virginia's Natural Bridge is the remains of a collapsed limestone cavern.* **Far left:** *In the Blue Ridge province, where metamorphic rocks of nearly equal hardness dominate, drainage patterns tend to be like the veins on a leaf. Drainage patterns in the Valley and Ridge province, however, follow easily-eroded rock layers—resulting in many parallel drainages.*

Facing page: *Cades Cove, Great Smoky Mountains National Park, is a geological window where older rocks—originally pushed over younger rocks by thrust faults—have eroded to expose the younger rocks beneath them.*

23

NEW RIVER, OLD RIVER

D espite its name, the New River is a very ancient water-way that cut its way through the Appalachian Mountains even as they were uplifted. The headwaters of the river are in North Carolina near the Tennessee border. From there the river flows in a generally northwest direction, across the Valley and Ridge and Appalachian Plateau provinces to its confluence with the Gauley River. Joined, the Gauley and New rivers become the Kanawha River, a tributary of the Ohio.

Its generally south-to-north flow reflects its antiquity. At one time the New River ran north into the St. Lawrence River drainage. However, during the last Ice Age, the New River's course was diverted by advancing ice sheets, which blocked its old channel north to Canada. Eventually its waters were captured by the Ohio.

A 52-mile stretch of the New River Gorge between Hinton and Fayetteville in West Virginia is classified as a National River and managed by the National Park Service. Nearby tributaries of the New River, the Gauley and Bluestone rivers, have also been given protection with designation as National Recreation Area and National Scenic River, respectively.

Right: On the New River Gorge National River, West Virginia.

Facing page: The New River, one of the oldest river systems in North America, once drained northward into the St. Lawrence River. Its channel was cut through the rising Appalachians.

3

WILDLIFE

JOHN SERRAO

Above: *Thirty-four species of salamander live in the Southern Appalachians; here, the spotted salamander.*

Facing page: *Red fox, shy and seldom seen by people.*

DIVERSITY & RESTORATION

You have to think small and look under logs and up into the trees to truly appreciate the wildlife of the Southern Appalachians. Long gone are many of the celebrated larger animals like bison, elk, wolf and, officially, mountain lion. Yes, there are still black bears and deer but, for the most part, the wildlife of the Southern Appalachians requires a careful eye and patient observation. Once this appreciative eye is developed, there is much to see.

SALAMANDERS

There are, for example, 34 species of salamanders in the Southern Appalachians, more than in any comparable area of the world. Many biologists believe the region is the center for salamander evolution. In terms of sheer numbers, salamanders are the most common vertebrate in the Southern Appalachians and, as a group, may be among the most voracious predators. In terms of prey, most salamanders will eat anything smaller than themselves, including worms, insects, beetles and almost any other small creeping creature. Their importance to ecological functions has been, until recently, overlooked by many.

Salamanders, as amphibians, rely upon moisture to keep from drying out and they usually lay their eggs in water or at least in very damp areas. Given the high annual precipitation found in the Southern Appalachians, it is not surprising that this region is such a significant area for salamanders. During the day, salamanders hide under rocks,

rotten logs or, for the aquatic varieties, in streams. Some, like the pygmy salamander, climb trees. The red-backed salamander is widely distributed, but others, like the red-cheeked salamander found only in Great Smoky Mountains National Park, appear in limited areas.

The many species of salamanders reflect the isolating influence of mountains. Many species cannot move easily from one mountain region to another, and they evolve in isolation. In a sense, each mountain region becomes an island of suitable habitat separated by miles of less suitable country. Over time, salamanders with a common ancestor will evolve into separate species.

ELEVATION ISLANDS

Another island effect of elevation is readily observed by the distribution of a number of Southern Appalachian species. Higher mountains form a southern extension of habitat for many cold-adapted species otherwise confined to northern climates. For instance, the nocturnal northern flying squirrel, an endangered species, is dependent upon the spruce-fir and high-elevation northern hardwood forests—typically above 5,000 feet. The northern flying squirrel population and range were severely reduced during the early logging days when many high-elevation forests were logged or burned.

Flying squirrels are usually found in older, more mature forests with plenty of snags and downed timber—what foresters used to call "decadent" but now label "old growth." The squirrels glide easily through the widely spaced trees, use the snags for nesting, and eat primarily fungi and lichens, not nuts or acorns like the more common gray squirrel. One reason for the dependency on old-growth spruce-fir forests is the abundance of fungi and mushrooms—one of their chief food resources.

The range of northern flying squirrels follows the high-

est ridges southward, and populations are restricted to small patches of suitable habitat on the highest mountains. Northern flying squirrels inhabit portions of the Monongahela National Forest in West Virginia, parts of the Jefferson and George Washington national forests in Virginia, and selected areas in the higher mountains of western North Carolina such Roan Mountain and Mt. Mitchell. The northern flying squirrel was recently reported in Great Smoky Mountains National Park after a 50-year hiatus.

Other northern species isolated in higher elevations include the flying squirrel's cousin, the red squirrel. Found in coniferous forests, the red squirrel is more active in daylight hours and in fact, often scolds hikers with noisy displeasure. The red squirrel is found as far south as northern Georgia. It also eats fungi, but seems to be most dependent upon the seeds from spruce, fir and pine cones. One can see these little squirrels in places like the Clingmans Dome area in the Great Smoky Mountains and at Grandfather Mountain and Mt. Mitchell in North Carolina.

Other northern species likely to be encountered at higher elevations, and usually in association with the spruce-fir or northern hardwood forests, include the water shrew, pygmy shrew, snowshoe hare, rock vole, fisher, New England cottontail and least weasel. But, like the northern flying squirrel, many of these species have shown a reduction in distribution and range, most likely due to the removal and fragmentation of high-elevation forests by turn-of-the-century logging practices. The snowshoe hare, for example, was once recorded for Great Smoky Mountains National Park, but is no longer found that far south. The water shrew also has suffered a loss in habitat. This shrew is very sensitive to stream sedimentation resulting from logging, road and highway construction.

The list of northern bird species found on higher mountains includes the ruffed grouse, black-capped chickadee, raven, saw-whet owl, red-breasted nuthatch, veery, black-throated green warbler, dark-eyed junco and golden-crowned kinglet.

AQUATIC ECOSYSTEMS

While the diversity of land-based animals may seem great, aquatic ecosystems offer even more niches for animals to fill. The waters of the Southern Appalachians have more species of fish than any other region of the country, and the Tennessee River in particular has more species than any other river in North America. For instance, New England has only 26 species of fish, but more than 300 species inhabit these southern mountains. Great Smoky Mountains National Park alone has 70 species of fish.

Many of these fish species are little known except to ichthyologists and as a consequence lack a constituency to lobby for their protection. Unfortunately, many fish species are disappearing due to pollution, habitat alteration and competition from non-native species. Of 20 endemic fish species in the Southern Appalachians, 11 are considered threatened or endangered and very likely will become extinct without some changes in the way we treat waterways. Endemic species are those native, or restricted to, a particular place.

The most famous of these local endemic fish is the snail darter, which had one of its few small remaining habitat areas destroyed by the construction of the Tellico Dam project, a boondoggle pork barrel construction project that has realized few of the benefits it would supposedly produce. A small population of snail darters was established in the Hiwassee River in Tennessee and appears to be holding its own.

Another fish sharing the snail darter's plight is the spotfin chub. This small fish prefers large clean rivers. Once found in 12 tributaries of the Tennessee River, its range has shrunk to only four drainages—the Little Tennessee, Duck, Emory and Holston rivers. It is listed as a federal Endangered Species. Extirpated from Great Smoky Mountains National Park by 1957, the spotfin chub has recently been reintroduced into Abrams Creek.

There is as much danger of extinction due to habitat fragmentation in aquatic ecosystems as in terrestrial ones. Dams, sewage pollution, river channelization, acid mine drainage and competition from other fish may effectively

Above: Chestnut-sided warbler.
Left top: Dead snags and trees are not a "wasted" resource, but an important habitat component for many species, including this eastern screech owl nesting in a large dead tree.
Left: Redback voles use downed logs as cover, hence are most common in old-growth forests.

Facing page: The nocturnal northern flying squirrel lives in cavities of hollow trees.

make some habitats unusable. Each of these can isolate native fish populations into smaller and smaller segments of rivers and streams. Without a reversal in trends, we will eventually lose entire populations and perhaps individual species.

While there are not many champions of the spotfin chub and snail darter, some fish—like the native brook trout of the southern highlands—have a host of supporters. A favorite of anglers, the native brook trout of the Southern Appalachians is restricted to clean, cold water habitat. Since colonial days the brook trout's range has declined significantly due to water pollution, sedimentation from logging and competition from non-native fish. The introduction of the rainbow trout, a species native to the western United States, and of the brown trout, originally from Germany, have eliminated brook trout from many lower-

elevation waters. Increasingly, the native trout is found only in the highest and smallest drainages.

A study that compared the distributional range of brook trout in 59 stream sections of Great Smoky Mountains National Park in 1935 with their known range in 1980 found nearly a 60 percent reduction. In all cases competition and expanding ranges of rainbow trout appeared to be the main causes for the brook trout decline. The only areas where brook trout populations appeared approximately the same were sections of streams above impassable waterfalls.

We tend to think of aquatic ecosystems in terms of fish, but they are the lifeblood for many non-aquatic species. They may seem a minor component of most terrestrial landscapes, but they nevertheless fuel much of the ecosystem. Many aquatic insects grow wings as mature adults and fly away. These insects then provide food for everything from bats to birds. Thus a decline in the quality of a waterway due to water pollution or sedimentation from logging can ripple through the entire food web.

RIPARIAN CREATURES

Other animals are very closely linked to riparian areas. For instance, the river otter, equipped with webbed feet and a streamlined body, is adept at capturing fish under water. Once found throughout the Southern Appalachians, the otter was trapped into local extinction over much of its natural range. Otters were gone from Great Smoky Mountains National Park by 1938, the year the park was created. By 1978, less than a hundred otters survived in all of Tennessee. Recently, nine were reintroduced into Great Smoky Mountains National Park and at least two have crossed the mountains into North Carolina.

Another water-loving mammal is the beaver. With a flattened tail and webbed feet, the beaver is a good swimmer. But unlike the otter, the beaver is strictly a vegetarian whose food preference includes the bark of black birch, dogwood and other species. As with the otter, unrestricted trapping decimated populations of these animals. By 1880, there were no beaver left in eastern Tennessee. Beavers were reintroduced in a number of southern Appalachian areas and, with protection, have begun to recolonize portions of their natural range.

CREATURES OF THE AIR

The slow increase of these animals is in contrast to the decline in other Southern Appalachian species. For instance, many bat species are declining and some are even threatened with extinction over much of their range. Within the Southern Appalachians, the gray bat, Indiana bat, and small-footed myotis are all threatened with extinction.

Reasons for the decline are many. Bats roost and hibernate in caves. Commercialism of caves, disturbance by spelunkers and even the killing of bats by vandals all contribute to the decline. Most bats have low reproductive capaci-

ROBERT C. SIMPSON PHOTOS

Above: *Interior forest species songbirds—like this black and white warbler—are disappearing as their habitat is fragmented.*
Right: *The bobcat is a common predator of the Southern Appalachians.*

Facing page: *Black bears need large patches of secure habitat to survive. Unless the remaining undeveloped roadless terrain in the Southern Appalachians is protected against further encroachment, bear numbers may decline dramatically.*

ties, producing only one young annually. They can not tolerate high population losses.

While some bats survive the cold winter months by migrating southward, many hibernate for the winter in caves. Bats are especially vulnerable during hibernation. If disturbed, they expend precious stored energy necessary to keep them alive through the winter. One arousal will burn as much fat as a bat would otherwise use in two to three weeks. If disturbed too frequently, bats can starve to death before insects become available again in the spring.

Other factors for bat declines include the widespread use of pesticides. Bats eat insects; in areas of heavy spraying, bats gradually accumulate poisons from their prey. Bats also may be dependent upon old-growth timber. For instance, loose bark on large shagbark hickory trees was found to harbor several mature colonies of the rare Indiana bat.

Many of the same factors that contribute to the decline in bats affect bird species as well. Many bird species need large contiguous patches of mature forest to successfully nest and rear young. As the forest is fragmented, forest songbird populations decline due to greater predation losses from raccoons, blue jays and snakes—as well as nest parasitism from brown-headed cowbirds. Interior-forest–dependent species like the yellow-throated vireo, northern parula, ovenbird, American redstart, black and white warbler, Louisiana waterthrush, and worm-eating warbler have declined dramatically as forest fragmentation has accelerated in both their summering grounds in North America and their wintering grounds in Central America.

The Great Smoky Mountains represent one of the largest unfragmented forest ecosystems in the Southern Appalachians. Their value as a natural ecological laboratory is immense. Research conducted in 1983 by ecologist Dave Wilcove demonstrates the value of large intact ecosystems. Wilcove wanted to determine if the observed decline of interior-forest songbirds was due to habitat fragmentation or other causes. Wilcove conducted a bird survey of a transect that had been surveyed in 1947 and 1948, and compared the species seen then with the birds there now. He found no evidence for songbird decline within the park. Interestingly, despite nine weeks of fieldwork, Wilcove did not record one brown-headed cowbird inside the park. Cowbirds are an indicator of forest fragmentation. They can substantially reduce songbird populations because they remove eggs or young from songbird nests and then lay their own eggs there. The unsuspecting songbirds raise the young cowbird as if it were their own.

Wilcove's study, among others, demonstrates the importance of large intact forest ecosystems. Serious migrant songbird population declines have been noted in forest patches 1,500 acres or less in size. It even has been demonstrated that roads create corridors that aid in the dispersal of nest parasites like the cowbird. Many biologists believe that logging roads and clearcutting or even selective cutting may jeopardize forest-interior-dependent species. If these birds continue to decline, it may be necessary to halt all logging or other disturbance on large blocks of public lands to ensure that adequate patches of mature forest stands remain. These findings run contrary to standard forestry and wildlife dicta, which for a generation or more taught that creating "edge" effect benefited all wildlife. We may in fact be edging many wildlife species to extinction.

BLACK BEAR AND ITS HABITAT

Another Southern Appalachian animal dependent upon large habitat patches and old mature forests is the black bear. Most black bears prefer to den in hollow trees and old snags, sometimes as much as 50 feet off the ground. One report documents a black bear denning in an old snag 100 feet off the ground. Obviously, to accommodate an animal as large as a bear, the trees have to be fairly good size. They also have to die. Modern forestry practices that cut trees before they are neither large nor dead pose a threat to the continued success of black bears in the region.

Sufficiently large blocks of habitat are important for security cover. Large road networks and habitat fragmentation accompanying logging and other developments make bears more vulnerable both to legal hunting and poaching. Poaching, in particular, poses a real threat to the bear's sur-

ROBERT C. SIMPSON

American redstart, among the bird species dependent on interior forests.

was established in 1936, only two bears were thought to live in the area. Today an estimated 600 to 800 bears reside in this one enclave—the densest black bear population in the United States. Bears are not endangered anywhere in the Southern Appalachians at present. An estimated 400 to 600 bears live in Great Smoky Mountains National Park and another 700 to 800 are thought to live in North Georgia. The mountainous portions of Tennessee, West Virginia, North Carolina and Virginia all have black bear populations.

However, the long-term viability of these populations is questionable. Research on the impacts of interstate highways on bear migrations and movements has shown that heavy traffic can deter the intermixing of bear populations. As more secure habitat patches are removed by logging, subdivisions and other development, bear populations may plummet.

Under ordinary circumstances, bears are not a threat to people. However, once they are habituated to people, and particularly to obtaining food from people, they can be dangerous. Between 1960 and 1980, nearly 90 percent of the black bear-human encounters involved bears habituated to human food and presence.

Without human foods to eat, black bears normally consume a wide variety of foods. In spring, bears eat grasses, leafy greens and a small, low-growing woodland plant called squawroot. In the fall acorns and other nuts are consumed. The larvae of yellowjackets and ants are favorite foods and important sources of protein. Although bears are 90 percent vegetarian, they will eat a wide variety of meats when available, including frogs, salamanders and carrion.

RETURN OF THE DEER

Besides bears, deer are the only other large mammal one is likely to see in the Southern Appalachians. Deer are one species that increases with forest fragmentation, and they have benefited from the intermix of farms and forest. Deer are fairly common today, so it's difficult to believe that even they were almost extirpated from the region. The extermination process began with the early settlers who of-

vival. A growing black market for bear gallbladders, used in Oriental traditional medicinal practices, is fueling the poaching epidemic. In 1989 alone, a U.S. Fish and Wildlife investigation yielded 43 indictments for bear poaching in North Carolina and Tennessee alone. Even national parks are not a safe haven for bears. Officials believe poachers killed more than 320 bears in Great Smoky Mountains National Park between 1985 and 1988.

Bears have a relatively low reproductive rate compared to other animals. Most females don't breed until they are three to four years old and they produce a litter of two cubs only every two years thereafter. Consequently loss of habitat, poaching, and excessive hunting pressure can pose a major threat to bear numbers. However, with habitat protection and forest maturation, bear numbers have increased. For instance, when Shenandoah National Park

ten supplemented their incomes by killing deer and selling their hides. Daniel Boone, for example, collected more than 2,000 deer hides during one of his hunting trips to Kentucky. Deer were also hunted for food and by the late 1800s they were relatively rare throughout the region, with local populations completely extinct in some areas. So rare were these animals that deer had to be reintroduced into what would be Shenandoah National Park in 1934. Today more than 6,000 deer are thought to roam the park.

DISAPPEARANCES

Of the larger mammals, many that once thrived here now are gone. A species of woods bison grazed the balds of Great Smoky Mountains National Park. Their trails followed the Great Valley from the Cumberland Valley of Pennsylvania through the Shenandoah Valley into Tennessee, and they are reported to have moved north each summer and south for winter. The shaggy beasts, never numerous, were gone from the Southern Appalachians by 1760, extirpated by Indians, who had acquired firearms. In the north, the bison held on a little longer, but the white settlers quickly slaughtered what the Indians missed.

Elk lasted a bit longer. Elk disappeared from North Carolina about the same time as bison, but hung on in Virginia until the mid-1800s. Several attempts to reintroduce elk have had limited success. Some elk were reintroduced in the Peaks of Otter area in Virginia's portion of the Blue Ridge Parkway in 1917, and more were added in 1935. However, they gradually disappeared due to poaching, disease, and perhaps problems caused by in-breeding.

Another rare or extinct animal that always inspires debate is the cougar. Panther and mountain lion are other names for this animal. Cougars once ranged over more of the western hemisphere than any other animal, from New Brunswick down to Florida and from British Columbia south through the American West and down into South America. The cougar was exterminated from much of its eastern range and today the only place in the eastern seaboard where they definitely are found is in Florida. Although cougars were killed by settlers simply because they

PHOTOS BY KEN LAYMAN/PHOTO AGORA

Above and left: *Overhunting once nearly removed deer from the Southern Appalachians. With the protection of game laws, their numbers have risen, and today they are relatively abundant.*

Above: *Red-tailed hawks are at home on natural savannahs or farmlands.*
Right: *The red-shouldered hawk favors moist river bottoms.*

Researcher Robert Downing spent two years checking records and sign throughout the region and has turned up only three individual instances where he believes the evidence strongly suggests the presence of a cougar. In most instances where photos or casts of "cougar" tracks have been made and shown to Downing, they have turned out to be prints made by dogs, bears or bobcats. Nevertheless, reports from what Downing believes are competent observers have come from Great Smoky Mountains National Park, Shenandoah National Park, Cohutta Wildlife Management area in north Georgia, and along the Blue Ridge Parkway near Mt. Pisgah. Does the cougar survive in the Southern Appalachians? Or, as Downing thinks, are some of the sightings of pet cougars released to fend for themselves in the wild? No one really knows.

Wildlife advocates discuss restoring many of the now-missing native species like the cougar to the Southern Appalachians. Sufficient prey base exists and the cougar could probably exist in many of the less developed parts of the region. Cougars range within a few miles of western cities like Boulder, Colorado and Missoula, Montana. There is no reason why they could not live in the Southern Appalachians. If no native cougars exist, western animals could be released in suitable habitats.

Like the predators, some of the larger mammals could be locally reestablished. For instance, bison—instead of cows—could be used to graze Cades Cove and the high-elevation balds of Great Smoky Mountains National Park. Although elk reintroductions have largely been a failure, with more animals there is a chance elk could survive in our larger wilderness areas like the Cranberry Wilderness in West Virginia, Shenandoah National Park or within the Great Smoky Mountains.

Whether the future is brighter with the reestablishment of native species or whether we continue to lose our native fauna, largely depends upon how we treat the landscape. Most animals are fairly resilient. With just a little care, the Southern Appalachians could remain a center for biological diversity and become a model for ecosystem restoration.

were predators, the near extinction of the whitetail deer, the cougar's chief prey species, probably accounts as much for their extinction.

There have, nevertheless, continued to be reports of cougar sightings throughout the Southern Appalachians. However, there is yet to be a substantiated find of a dead or live animal. In Florida, where no more than 50 or 60 cougars are thought to survive, 10 to 15 are hit and killed by cars on highways each year. So, if cougars survive in the Southern Appalachians, why aren't more killed on the roads? No one has an answer. One thing is certain: cougars are very secretive. Yet it seems unlikely that any species could for decades elude detection or avoid being shot, hit by a car or otherwise die.

RED WOLF

MICHAEL HALMINSKI

The red wolf once inhabited lower elevations in the Southern Appalachians. The Fish and Wildlife Service, in conjunction with the National Park Service, is beginning a study to determine if Great Smoky Mountains National Park might be a suitable location for a red wolf reintroduction. The wolf's howl may be heard here again.

Historically the red wolf ranged throughout the Southeast United States, while the gray wolf, a separate species from the smaller red, roamed the Southern Appalachians as well as much of the northern and western portions of North America. But poisoning and trapping programs nearly extirpated the species. In the late 1960s, only a handful of red wolves were left in the world. Some 40 genetically pure individuals found in east Texas and nearby Louisiana were taken into captivity in the 1970s. Their numbers increased to 105 by 1989, with 14 now living in the wild again at the Alligator River National Wildlife Refuge in North Carolina, as well as on several offshore islands.

Unlike gray wolves, red wolves do not usually attack or eat large prey like deer, but tend to capture smaller prey like rabbits, mice, opossum and insects.

Even if it is introduced, most park visitors are unlikely to see a red wolf. They are very shy creatures and generally nocturnal. Unlike the gray wolf that may form large packs, the red wolf usually travels alone or in pairs except for family groups. Just as with the gray wolf, the red wolf poses almost no threat to humans.

Like the successfully reintroduced red wolves in Alligator National Wildlife Refuge, red wolves reintroduced into the Smokies will wear radio collars so their movements can be monitored at all times. If they stray too far from the recovery area, they will be recaptured.

As part of the mandate to preserve all creatures and ecological processes, national parks are appropriate locations for reintroduction of extirpated species. If reintroduced, the red wolf almost certainly would surpass the black bear as the animal most park visitors hope to see. It would indeed be a treat if the red wolf once again roamed the coves and hollows of the Southern Appalachians.

Left: *The red wolf, a separate species from the gray wolf, once inhabited the southeast U.S. from Texas to North Carolina.*

4

FLORA

AWE-INSPIRING FORESTS

Above: *Mountain laurel, a common spring flower.*

Facing page: *Mountain laurel and pines on the Chattahoochee National Forest, Georgia.*

Trees. Trees so abundant that the natural moisture and terpenes given off by their respiration contribute to the smoky or blue haze immortalized in such Southern Appalachian names as Great Smoky Mountains and Blue Ridge. If there is one natural attribute of the region that commands attention and awe, it is the forests. Beginning as early as 1775, when the American botanist William Bartram first surveyed and collected plants in the Southern Appalachians and spoke of their "sublime magnificence," American naturalists have celebrated the region's floral wonders.

Bartram spent five years on extended plant collecting trips in the Southeast, including several years exploring the mountains of western North Carolina. Bartram was followed in the late 1700s by Andre and Francois Michaux, a father and son team from France. Based in Charleston, South Carolina, the Michauxs spent much of their time in the mountains of western North Carolina, including trips into the Great Smoky Mountains, Grandfather Mountain and Black Range. The Oconee bell was found among their collections by Harvard botanist Dr. Asa Gray. Gray was able to relocate the plant at last in 1877. He left his name on a rare beauty—the Gray's lily—an endemic that grows only in this region. For botanists eager to discover new species, the Southern Appalachians were fertile hunting grounds.

More than a hundred years after Bartram and other early botanists had tramped the Southern Appalachian forests, another major figure in American conservation history visited the region. Gifford Pinchot, founder of the U.S. Forest Service, obtained his first job as a practicing forester on George Vanderbilt's Biltmore estate near Asheville, North Carolina. Pinchot was enthusiastic about these forests. He wrote, "Nowhere else in America were there so many kinds of trees, nowhere else in the East mountains so high, forests so gorgeous, trees so huge as in this Southern Appalachian region."

ASTOUNDING VARIETY

Despite massive clearing of the forests for farms, lumbering and other development, Pinchot's assertion that the Southern Appalachian forests had superlative qualities are as true today as they were a hundred years ago. The sheer diversity of species is astounding—more than 130 species of trees, a number greater than found in all of northern Europe. In addition, there are some 2,400 other plant species including 1,500 flowers, shrubs, mosses and lichens—more varieties than found in any comparably sized area in North America! The flora of the Southern Appalachians are a living remnant of what was once a vast forest that covered much of the earth millions of years ago. It represents a national treasure trove for biological diversity that is only beginning to be appreciated.

Biologists frequently refer to the Southern Appalachians as one of two major centers for biological diversity in North America. There are three major reasons why the region has such a diversity of species. First, the generally mild, moist climate is favorable to plant growth. Furthermore, the Southern Appalachians escaped Ice Age glaciation and, as a consequence, remained a refugium for species dislocated from the north. Many disjunct locations for northern plants occur in the Southern Appalachians. For

GEORGE WUERTHNER PHOTOS BOTH PAGES

Above: Flowering dogwood in a cove hardwood forest.
Right: Silverbell is a species endemic to the Southern Appalachians.

Facing page, left: Old-growth forest of eastern hemlock and yellow poplar in Shenandoah National Park, Virginia.
Inset: Blossom of the yellow poplar, or tulip tree.

GEORGE WUERTHNER PHOTOS

instance, the occurrence of red spruce, a northern tree species on high mountains of the Great Smoky Mountains and elsewhere in the Southern Appalachians, is just one example of a northern tree species that migrated southward during the last Ice Age and found a home in the region. Bog rose, a plant common in Canada and New England sphagnum bogs, is found in isolated wetland sites as far south as North Carolina. Finally, the region is biologically diverse because the great elevational differences created by mountains provide many climatic zones and thus a wide variety of habitats.

Although many of the region's plant species are found in several geographical regions of the country, there are at least 200 species native only to the Southern Appalachians, including the aforementioned Oconee bell and Gray's lily, white-fringed phacelia and silverbell.

This great plant diversity tends to be dictated by the larger tree species commonly found growing together. Although there are various classifications, many biologists recognize five major forest types in the Southern Appalachians: cove hardwood, oak-hickory-chestnut, spruce-fir, northern hardwood, and oak-pine.

COVE HARDWOOD FORESTS

Of the five, perhaps the most memorable is the cathedral cove hardwood. Cove hardwood forests grow on deep soils in the lower to middle elevations—up to 4,500 feet. The most notable cove hardwood species is the stately and often massive yellow poplar, or tulip tree. Specimens sometimes grow to heights of more than 200 feet. Growing alongside yellow poplar are eastern hemlock, basswood, black cherry, sugar maple, American beech, yellow buckeye and silverbell. In fact, the cove hardwood is the most diverse forest type in North America. More than 80 tree species are associated with it, and well beyond 50 tree species have been found in one cove hardwood stand.

Many tree species reach their greatest size on these favorable sites. In cove hardwood forests within Great Smoky Mountains National Park 600-year-old trees reach amazing girths. One yellow poplar in the Cosby area has a circum-

40

ference of 27 feet; an eastern hemlock near the Roaring Fork is nearly 20 feet around. Clearly, these are giants among trees and approach the size of the celebrated giant conifers of the Pacific Northwest.

However, size is not the only characteristic these woodlands share with the better known Pacific Northwest forests. Mature cove hardwood forests also display marvelous examples of old-growth forest characteristics similar to those noted for the giant coniferous forests of the West Coast—including many snags, downed logs and a multi-canopy forest. Because the larger trees of the canopy intercept light and use up much of the moisture, the floor in such forests tends to be rather open with widely spaced trees that appear like pillars holding up a leafy green roof.

Cove hardwood forests are places of serenity where lime-green light filters through a many-layered canopy and the air remains cool and refreshing even on warm summer days. The largest trees in the Southern Appalachians are found in these favorable growing sites. As a result of logging, they are now among the rarest of the major forest types. Nevertheless, a number of good examples are found in Great Smoky Mountains National Park, including along the upper Laurel Falls Trail and Ramsey Cascade Trail. The Joyce Kilmer Memorial Forest of the Nantahala-Pisgah National Forest is another fine example of cove hardwood forest.

The loss of the large virgin cove hardwood forests is apparent to anyone who visits the few remaining old-growth groves. There are other subtle, long-term changes attributable to timber harvest as well. Great Smoky Mountains National Park drainages logged prior to the park's establishment 70 or more years ago show notable differences from similar but unlogged drainages. Unlogged drainages had higher levels of nutrients important to aquatic ecosystems, including nitrates, sulfate, phosphate, calcium, magnesium and organic carbon.

Another significant difference between logged and unlogged drainages is the amount of woody debris—logs and branches—that ultimately winds up in the streams. In one study, unlogged drainages had four times as much woody

GEORGE WUERTHNER

JOHN SERRAO

41

Above: *American chestnut once dominated the forests of the Southern Appalachians, but a blight introduced from the Orient killed all the mature trees.*
Right: *So resistant to decay is chestnut wood that old stumps, some more than 50 years old, still can be found in these forests.*

Facing page: *Chestnut oaks along the Blue Ridge Parkway.*

debris and 10 times the debris-dams of logged drainages. Since woody debris is important for the long-term nutrient flow in aquatic ecosystems and is a major factor in creating fish habitat and stabilizing stream channels, the significantly lower amounts in logged drainages make questionable the idea that forest ecosystems can be "sustained" in the face of repeated timber harvest. This study is just one example of the importance of keeping our remaining virgin cove hardwood forests as pristine "control" areas, against which human impacts and manipulation of the environment can be measured.

OAK-HICKORY-CHESTNUT FOREST

Today the cove hardwood forests are the premier forest stands of the region; at one time, however, the oak-hickory-chestnut association may have rivaled them for magnificence. The dominant tree of this association was American chestnut, sometimes composing 75 percent of the forest. It was a giant, reaching diameters of more than 17 feet and towering more than 100 feet into the forest canopy. The tree was perhaps the most important one in the Southern Appalachian forests, producing durable rot-resistant wood for settlers and dependable supplies of chestnuts that fed wildlife from turkey to black bear. Then, in 1904, an exotic fungus lethal to mature American chestnuts was introduced from the Orient. By 1930, the disease had killed most of the chestnuts in Virginia and had reached western North Carolina; by the 1950s, few mature trees remained alive.

The bark and wood of chestnut is full of natural preservatives and so resistant to rot that it is still possible to walk through the Southern Appalachian forests and come upon old chestnut logs. Although the chestnut blight kills mature trees, the species survived because it sends up sprouts from roots. As a result, the long, narrow, toothed leaf is still rather common on understory growth throughout the region.

There is hope that the American chestnut will again take its place in the forest. New genetic research is crossing blight-resistant strains of Chinese chestnut with American chestnut. This hybrid is again crossed back with American chestnut several more times, making a tree that is 98 percent American chestnut, but nevertheless invulnerable to the blight.

The oak-hickory-chestnut forest type is generally associated with drier sites that have shallower soils than those supporting the cove hardwoods. As a consequence, it is more common in the drier northern part of Virginia, as well as on ridges and other areas where soils are thinner. Oak-chestnut is the most common forest type on the George Washington National Forest and in Shenandoah National Park. Indicators of this drier regime are the oaks—northern red, white, chestnut oak, black and scarlet—plus white pine, hickory, sourwood and black walnut.

The abundance of nuts in this forest type makes it very important for wildlife. The nuts, called mast, provide food for squirrels, deer, turkeys, ruffed grouse, black bears and a host of other creatures. Even ducks will feed on acorns found in streams and ponds. So important is mast in the diets of many animals that breeding success in any particular year is largely determined by the yield of nuts.

A healthy chestnut produces good nut crops nearly every year. Other mast producers are less regular and, unfortunately for wildlife, some years the crops fail. Failure seems related to the earlier flowering of oaks versus chestnuts. Late frosts can kill the flowers on oaks, while chestnuts typically flower in early June when the threat of frost is almost nonexistent. White oak, a common Southern Appalachian hardwood species, produces approximately 1,000 acorns per mature tree.

OAK-PINE FOREST

On the driest sites—sandy soils or rocky knobs—one finds oak-pine forests. Several oaks tolerant of drier environments—including the black, chestnut and scarlet oaks—are found intermixed with pines. Understory plants include such shrubs as rosebay rhododendron and mountain laurel.

The pines, in particular, are very drought resistant, hence tend to dominate. Again, dry areas of the George

LARRY ULRICH

43

Washington National Forest as well as rain shadow areas in North Carolina (such as around Asheville), tend to have a greater number of pines.

Southern Appalachian pines include Virginia pine, Table Mountain pine, pitch pine, shortleaf pine and eastern white pine. The white pine achieves relatively large size, but the others tend to be smaller, and a few—such as pitch pine—are even brushy in appearance.

One reason pines are common on well drained or dry sites is their ability to conserve water. Their needles have a waxy coating that helps resist water losses. This is one reason why, in the drought-prone western United States, conifers, rather than deciduous hardwoods, dominate.

Nearly all the Southern Appalachian pines are adapted to periodic fire and are resistant to injuries from ground fires. Some, like Table Mountain pine, actually thrive in the face of repeated fires because their cones tend to remain closed until opened by intense heat. After a fire, the cones inundate a recently burned site with seeds. Nearly all pines grow best in open sunlight—the condition that prevails after a burn.

Prior to modern fire suppression, fires were more common in the Southern Appalachian forests, largely as a result of human activities. Prior to white settlement, Virginia's Shenandoah Valley was a vast prairie kept open by fires set annually by the Indians. This annual firing kept the woodlands from invading the prairie, which attracted grass-eating big game like bison and elk—species the Indians hunted. The Spanish explorer De Soto traveled through the Southern Appalachians on horseback accompanied by herds of livestock, indicating that frequent fires kept the woods relatively open.

Even after whites settled in the mountains, frequent fires were the rule, not the exception. Settlers burned the woods to favor grasses eaten by their livestock. A 1905 survey of more than 6.5 million acres of Southern Appalachian forests found 80 percent of the trees bore scars from repeated fires.

Prior to active fire suppression, fires burned through pine forests in the Great Smoky Mountains about every 12

GEORGE WUERTHNER

years, particularly on drier south slopes. As a result of suppression, pine forests are gradually being replaced by more shade-tolerant hardwood species.

Lightning occasionally causes fires in the Southern Appalachians, but most fires here are of human origin. Between 1940 and 1979, 87 percent of fires in Great Smoky Mountains National Park were started by people; nearly half were acts of arson by locals.

The susceptibility to fire damage of individual tree species varies considerably. Among hardwoods, yellow poplar is more resistant than any of the oaks. Chestnut oak is more resistant to fires than white oak, while scarlet oak is the most vulnerable to fire-related injuries. Nevertheless, oaks in particular are less susceptible to root-kill by fires, thus fire may be an important factor in promoting successful oak regeneration.

Pines are usually more resistant to low-intensity fires than hardwoods, but most hardwoods readily resprout from roots after their above-ground parts are burned. Sprouters include oak, black cherry, red maple, dogwood, blackgum, sourwood and basswood.

The Indians set prairie fires annually to keep land open for bison and elk.

Left: *Acorns are a rich source of protein and a critically important food for a wide variety of wildlife.*

Facing page, left: *Sourwood and red maple.*
Right top: *Sassafras leaves.*
Bottom: *Large old-growth white pine. Pines tend to be found on drier sites such as ridges, or sandy and well drained soils.*

45

FREDERICK D. ATWOOD

Above: *Birch leaves.*
Right: *Fraser fir. Firs have upright cones that gradually fall apart while on the tree, so one seldom find whole fir cones on the ground.*

Facing page: *Moss and lichens cloak the forest floor beneath a red spruce forest.*

JOHN ELK III

NORTHERN HARDWOOD FOREST

At higher elevations, the greater precipitation, cloud cover and generally cooler, moister conditions result in fewer fires and favor northern hardwoods. As their name suggests, these are tree species one is likely to find in New England. Dominated by yellow birch, sugar maple and American beech, these forests offer the most intense and colorful autumn leaf displays, while the moist, rich soils favor wildflower displays in spring.

SPRUCE-FIR FOREST

Dark, green islands, spruce-fir forests cap the tops of the highest mountain summits above 4,500 feet—little bits of Canada moved south to the mountains of the Southern Appalachians. The climate at these elevations is nearly as extreme as in northern New England. Temperatures as low as 34 degrees below zero have been recorded on several

Southern Appalachian mountain tops, and snow is not uncommon. Growing under these extreme conditions are the red spruce and Fraser fir. The fir is slightly better adapted to the harshest conditions and comprises a larger percentage of the forest at higher elevations.

Perhaps the most notable characteristic of these forests is their evergreen quality. In the harsher, cooler, high-mountain environment where conifers survive, growing seasons are short. Conifers retain their needles for several years, rather than losing them each fall. They can begin manufacturing food immediately whenever conditions are favorable for growth, without having to delay production to produce a new set of leaves like hardwoods. High-elevation conifers like spruce and fir have a pointed "Christmas tree" shape, which helps them shed snow.

This forest type is perhaps the rarest of the major communities found in the Southern Appalachian mountains, with only seven mountainous areas recording any significant acreage of the spruce-fir forest type. A recent survey by the U.S. Forest Service found only 65,700 acres in the entire region. And 74 percent of all spruce-fir forest in the entire Southern Appalachians is found in Great Smoky Mountains National Park. The Black Mountains, which include Mt. Mitchell, have the next greatest amount with 11 percent, followed by the Balsam Mountains, 10 percent; Roan Mountain, 2 percent; Mt. Rogers, 2 percent; and Grandfather Mountain, 1 percent. Mt. Rogers is the northern limit of Fraser fir, which is there replaced by balsam fir, a species more typical of New England. Other scattered and isolated pure spruce stands or spruce-fir forests on other mountain uplands include Spruce Knob in West Virginia and some of the higher peaks in Shenandoah National Park, like Stony Man and Hawksbill Mountain.

But all is not well with the spruce-fir forest. Dead silvery snags are the dominant feature of the higher elevations of Mt. Mitchell, Clingmans Dome or along the ridgetop of the Balsam Mountains on the Blue Ridge Parkway. Of the total acreage of spruce-fir forest in the Southern Appalachians, 24 percent is dead or nearly dead. Most of these dead trees are Fraser fir, and studies show that as much as

95 percent of the fir in Great Smoky Mountains National Park is already dead. Other areas are affected less severely.

The death of Fraser fir is attributed to the balsam woolly adelgid, an exotic insect introduced from Europe. It was discovered first in Shenandoah National Park in 1956. Injury to fir results when saliva from the adelgid stimulates a rapid cancer-like cell division within the tree's cambium layer. The resulting woody substance blocks the passage of water and minerals between the tree roots and crown.

Fraser fir face extinction if all the mature cone-bearing trees die. In a few places, most notably Great Smoky Mountain National Park, efforts to save at least some mature Fraser fir are occurring. Each summer, park managers hand-spray some of the more accessible fir trees on Clingmans Dome with a biodegradable soap. The soap kills the balsam woolly adelgid. However, since a tree must be thoroughly covered with the soap mixture, only a very small percentage of the existing Fraser fir forest can be treated.

EFFECTS OF POLLUTION

The other major factor thought to be killing high-elevation forests is air pollution, which includes acid rain, atmospheric deposition of air-borne heavy metals, and other pollutants in rain or snow. Spruce-fir forests are particularly susceptible to such pollution because needles are more efficient at filtering pollutants from the air than are broad leaves. Secondly, there is simply more pollution deposition at higher elevations since mountain tops have more fog and mist, higher precipitation, and increased amounts of snow. In particular, pollutants trapped in snow can be released in a strong pulse of toxins when the snow melts in the spring.

Emissions from automobiles, and coal burning for electricity generation—among other factors—have increased significantly during the past few decades. These pollutants contribute to the formation of "acid rain." Ozone damage to the forest also has been detected. Whether acid rain and other pollutants are contributing factors in the susceptibility of Fraser fir to the balsam woolly adelgid only can be

Above *Roan Mountain, a grassy bald on the Tennessee-North Carolina border.*

Right: *Trillium, a common spring flower.*

speculated. However, a strong healthy tree has a greater chance of resisting infestations than a tree already weakened by air pollution and toxic metals. Although the impact of air pollution appears to be greatest at high elevations, a measurable decline in tree growth at all elevations has been detected throughout the South, and air pollution may be a contributing factor.

Acid rain may be the major cause of red spruce decline. Fourteen percent of spruces on Mt. Mitchell are already dead, and measurement of other still-living trees throughout the region has demonstrated that growth practically stopped in the early 1960s. This decline is manifested by the virtual cessation of new wood laid down in the tree's annual rings, as well as loss of branches and needles.

THE BALDS

Loss of the spruce-fir forest may slow the encroachment by trees into another unique Southern Appalachian plant community—the balds. Balds are meadow-like treeless openings within otherwise forested areas, which crown many of the higher peaks and ridges throughout the Southern Appalachian region. No one really knows how balds were created, although it is thought that a combination of fire and grazing may be responsible for their maintenance. Records show that Indians and settlers burned off these mountaintops and that large ungulates like bison and elk, later replaced by cattle and sheep, continued to keep encroaching shrubs and trees at bay.

In the absence of disturbance, particularly from fire, grazing animals or manual cutting of invading shrubs and trees, balds tend to become reforested. Natural fire is too infrequent to maintain these unique plant communities. Prescribed burning can prevent invasion of shrubs, but is ineffective if shrubs are already established, since plants like blackberries, blueberries, mountain laurel and rhododendron resprout from roots if burned. Some scientists believe that, without manipulation, all the balds within Great Smoky Mountains National Park will be forested within 30 to 70 years.

The vegetation of balds varies from location to location, but there are two commonly recognized varieties: grassy balds and heath balds. Grassy balds look like meadows and tend to be dominated by mountain oat grass, timothy, Kentucky bluegrass and a number of flowers like wild strawberry, dwarf cinquefoil and goldenrod.

Heath balds, also called slicks, tend to be dominated by evergreen shrubs like purple rhododendron, mountain laurel, highbush blueberry, flame azalea and bracken fern. Heath balds are less common than grassy balds.

Among the better known balds are Andrews Bald, Silers Bald, Parsons Bald and Gregory Bald in Great Smoky Mountains National Park; Standing Indian in the Nantahala National Forest; Big Bald Mountain in the Cherokee National Forest; Whitetop Mountain in the Jefferson National Forest; and Roan Mountain in the Pisgah National Forest.

RITES OF SPRING

People converge on the Southern Appalachians during the relatively short spring period when wildflowers are abundant. Great Smoky Mountains National Park, along with the Gatlinburg Garden Club, Southern Appalachian Botanical Club and the University of Tennessee, sponsor an annual Spring Wildflower Pilgrimage, usually at the end of April. The program offers conducted wildflower walks and motor tours that explain natural history as well as identification of important spring flowers.

Because of the great elevational and latitudinal range of the Southern Appalachians, something is usually in bloom from February, at lower elevations, to late summer and fall at higher elevations. The same flower species can vary its peak flowering period by as much as six weeks, depending upon elevation.

Early bloomers include hepatica, spring beauty and violets. These flowers bloom before leaves close the forest canopy. By early to mid-April, or around the time when the trees begin to sprout new leaves, the woods are dotted with white fringed phacelia, bluets, trillium and a host of other flowers. At this time of year, the flowering trees and shrubs bloom as well. From late April into May, flowering dogwood, flame azalea, Fraser magnolia, mountain silverbell, redbud and a host of other trees and shrubs brighten the forest gloom. By mid-June, the highest elevations are ablaze with the blossom of mountain laurel and purple Catawba rhododendron.

One of the most beautiful spring floral displays is the white-petaled flowering dogwood tree. Yet, like the Fraser fir and the American chestnut, the dogwood's days as a member of the Southern Appalachian flora may be numbered. A deadly fungus, known as dogwood anthracnose, is devastating dogwood populations throughout the South. Acid rain is also implicated. Laboratory studies have shown that the higher the acid content of rain, the greater the fungus damage.

Dogwood anthracnose was first detected in the Northeast and Pacific Northwest in the mid-1970s. It has since spread southward, and strikes trees that are stressed. In addition, trees close to mountain streams seem to be more vulnerable, apparently related to the high level of humidity that favors fungus growth.

Another exotic attacking the Southern Appalachian forests is the gypsy moth. The gypsy moth caterpillar defoliated 10 to 15 percent of the trees in Shenandoah National Park during the summer of 1989. Gypsy moths attack oaks, and the implications for wildlife are serious. Oaks are the dominant mast producers since the demise of the American chestnut. The oaks' defoliation also affects shade-loving plants like ginseng, which suffer under full sunlight.

Despite these setbacks from disease, logging, attacks from exotic insects and losses due to subdivision and development, the forests of the Southern Appalachians remain one of the region's leading drawing cards. Most residents and visitors are likely to agree with botanist William Bartram who, in 1776, called the Southern Appalachians "one of the most charming natural mountain landscapes perhaps anywhere to be seen..."

"...one of the most charming natural mountain landscapes perhaps anywhere to be seen..."
—William Bartram, 1776

CRADLE OF FORESTRY

Nowhere else in America had trees as magnificent as those in the Southern Appalachians, Gifford Pinchot decided in 1892, when he first visited the Biltmore estate near Asheville, North Carolina. Pinchot became the founder of the U.S. Forest Service.

In the late 1880s, usual timber harvest practices involved cutting the best timber—high-grading it is called—then burning the rest. Timber companies scoffed at the idea that one could ever come back and log a site a second time. The standard assumption was that once an area was logged, the company had to move to the next region and begin anew.

Gifford Pinchot, educated in European forestry schools—there were no schools of forestry in America at that time—meant to change these destructive practices. He believed in practicing good forestry as opposed to outright preservation. As he once wrote: "The job was not to stop the ax, but to regulate its use." Although such an idea seems almost second nature to us today, for his time and era, Pinchot was a radical, a rebel with a mission in life. Prior to Pinchot, there was no such thing as natural resource management, only exploitation. Pinchot was determined to change the face of natural resource utilization and to a great extent he succeeded.

Pinchot believed in setting an example rather than merely preaching. He began his crusade on the Vanderbilt estate. Using selective cutting methods, Pinchot and his assistants marked individual trees and, with great care, cut and removed them without damaging other trees. Pinchot was able to prove that careful logging practices, with an eye towards the future of the forest, could be profitable as well as beneficial to the land. At Pinchot's urgings,

Vanderbilt purchased more than 100,000 acres of land centered on Mt. Pisgah. Later, these Vanderbilt holdings would become the nucleus of the Pisgah National Forest.

Pinchot began a movement to change the administrative and legal policies of the vast holdings of federal lands, which then were primarily in the West. With the help of Theodore Roosevelt, his lifelong friend who became president, Pinchot established millions of acres of new national forests. In 1905, the U.S. Forest Service was created to manage these lands—with Pinchot as its first chief.

Dr. Carl Schenck took over Pinchot's position at Biltmore in 1895. Schenck started the first forestry school in the nation in 1897, in the Biltmore Forest. The school operated until 1914, and graduated 367 foresters who went on to practice the new and growing field of forestry throughout the United States.

Today, Pinchot's and Schenck's early experiments in forest management are explained at the "Cradle of Forestry in America," a national historical site of the Pisgah National Forest in North Carolina.

As in Pinchot's time, the Southern Appalachians today are where new directions in forestry are being shaped, as foresters, biologists and others initiate a new era recognizing that a forest is far more than a collection of trees. Gifford Pinchot would be pleased to know that forestry has become a major force in the conservation and preservation of natural resources.

Above: *Gifford Pinchot (left) and his friend, President Theodore Roosevelt, who shared his conservationist beliefs.*

Facing page: *Ferns along the Cataloochee Divide, Great Smoky Mountains National Park.*

5

HISTORY

Above: *An example of skilled Cherokee basket-making.*

Facing page: *The old Tipton place, Cades Cove, Great Smoky Mountains National Park.*

12,000 YEARS OF MAN

The Southern Appalachians have been inhabited more or less continuously for 12,000 years. The first people were Paleo-Indians—big-game hunters who stalked mastodons and other Ice Age mega-fauna. They had only spears—the bow would not be invented for thousands of years—and they moved frequently, concentrating their hunts on the larger mammals.

Then, about 10,000 years ago, the climate grew progressively warmer. Ice Age mammals died out—some scientists think they were extirpated as a result of overhunting by the Paleo-Indians. We may never know the full story, but we do know that native inhabitants of this region became more sedentary. Although hunting still was an important activity, wild fruits, nuts, vegetables and fish rounded out their diet.

This lifestyle continued for thousands of years until a new cultural period began about 2,800 years ago, with the advent of cultivation. Besides gathering wild foods, crops such as sunflower, marsh elder and squash all were grown in fields. It was only relatively recently, about 1,775 years ago, that maize, or corn, was introduced into the region.

The introduction of agriculture changed the way people lived as much or more than the internal combustion engine affected our own way of life. Agriculture allowed larger numbers of people to inhabit the region than could be sustained by hunting and gathering traditions. Large villages developed, walled by palisades as protection against enemy tribes. Religious ceremony became more elaborate and ceremonial mounds were built in the center of the larger villages in many parts of the southeast. The Indians cleared extensive tracts of river bottomlands, fragmenting the forest and increasing the amount of edge between field and woodland. This favored animals of the interface, like elk and deer, upon which the Indians came to rely as meat sources when they acquired the bow and arrow.

ARRIVAL OF THE CHEROKEE

About 1000 A.D., the Cherokee, an Indian tribe related to the Iroquois of New York, moved south from the upper Ohio River Valley and occupied the Southern Appalachians, establishing major villages in northern Georgia, eastern Tennessee and western North Carolina. The Cherokee farmed the river valleys and hunted the uplands. Their typical village had 40 to 50 log homes surrounded by protective log palisades, beyond which lay the agricultural fields.

In 1540, Spanish explorer Hernando de Soto passed through what would be western North Carolina and eastern Tennessee, the first European to traverse the region. De Soto visited the Cherokee as well as other tribes of the region and his party is probably responsible for introducing European diseases like smallpox. European diseases, rather than outright warfare, decimated the Indian people of North America. At the height of their power in the 1700s, Cherokee population is estimated to have been from 25,000 to 50,000. The people claimed as their territory the area from southwest Virginia to northern Georgia.

By the early 1700s, a brisk trade between South Carolina traders and the Cherokee was well established. In exchange for animal hides—including those of deer, bison, elk—the Indians obtained such European wares as pots, needles, blankets, axes and rifles.

Above: *This scene from the anthropologically-accurate outdoor drama "Unto These Hills" portrays the Cherokee eagle dance before a backdrop of reconstructed village palisades.*
Right: *A traditional Cherokee dance mask carved by Will West Long around 1940.*

Facing page: *Reconstructions of Cherokee structures of about 1750, at Oconaluftee Indian Village, show the interior of a council house **(left)** and a typical dwelling **(right)**.*

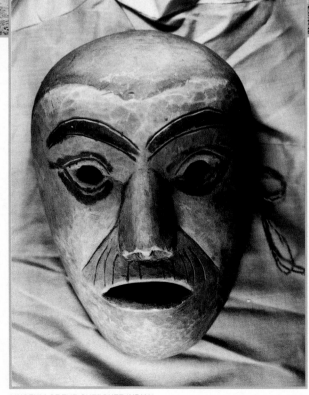

The fur trade was significant. By 1708, South Carolina reported exports of more than 50,000 skins. Evidence suggests that the rifles enabled Cherokee to extirpate bison from the Southern Appalachians prior to the region's settlement by whites.

WHITE SETTLERS FROM THE NORTH

Although the traders changed the way the Cherokee lived, whites did not pose a direct threat to Indian lands until the 1730s and 1740s, when frontier families began to settle the region. The majority of these settlers came from the north. Following the general southwest-northeast trend of the valleys, descendants of Scotch-Irish and German colonists moved south from Pennsylvania, first settling the Cumberland and Shenandoah valleys, then pouring into North Carolina's piedmont country. By 1745, there were more than 10,000 residents in the Shenandoah Valley and a short 20 years later more than 35,000 newcomers resided here, leaving little arable land unspoken for.

With vacant land scarce in Virginia, settlers moved farther south into North Carolina and eventually moved west of the mountains into Tennessee and Kentucky. Between 1732 and 1754, the population of North Carolina doubled. One of the families to settle the Yadkin River region of North Carolina was that of Squire Boone, whose son Daniel would become a major trailblazer of the Southern Appalachian region.

The fertile soils of the valleys, combined with waterpower from numerous rivers and an abundance of wild game, made this region particularly attractive to settlers. For many a frontier family, killing game not only put meat in the pot, but also supplied hides that were an important item of trade. For instance, in 1753, more than 30,000 deer hides were shipped from North Carolina alone. But deer were not the only animals in abundance. The journals of Dr. Thomas Walker, a surveyor for the Loyal Land Company, reported that while his party was employed in the Shenandoah Valley of Virginia, they killed "thirteen buffaloes, eight elks, fifty-three bears, twenty deer, four wild geese and about 150 turkeys."

At the same time that these British and American colonists were expanding south and west, the French were moving east from the Mississippi. However, the French were more interested in trade than in outright settlement. They set up trading posts among the Cherokee Indians in east Tennessee and, on occasion, attacked Cherokee towns whose sympathies remained with the British.

In response to the stepped-up French attacks, in 1753 the British built Fort Prince George in South Carolina and, in 1756, Fort Loudoun in Tennessee—partially to protect the Cherokee and partially to protect British borders and interests. The construction of Fort Loudoun was also an initial step in establishing settlements west of the mountains. However, friction between the British and Cherokee increased and, three years later, the governor of South Carolina declared war on the Cherokee. In response, the Cherokee captured Fort Loudoun. The soldiers were permitted to leave the fort, but later were attacked as they retreated to South Carolina. In retaliation, in 1761, Capt. James Grant and several thousand soldiers attacked and burned to the ground a number of Cherokee towns.

BOTH PHOTOS COURTESY MUSEUM OF THE CHEROKEE INDIAN

Above: *View of Cumberland Gap, a major pathway through the mountains between Kentucky and Virginia.*

Facing page: *Daniel Boone was one of the early white settlers of the mountainous parts of North Carolina, and later pioneered a major pathway into Kentucky via the "Wilderness Road" that passed through Cumberland Gap.*

Nevertheless, it was disputed territory and Kentucky was known as a "dark and bloody ground" because both the Shawnee and Cherokee hunted this no-man's land, and each tried to kill the other tribe's warriors at every opportunity. Perhaps because neither group occupied the region year-round, hunting pressure was lessened and game was abundant.

In 1750, Dr. Thomas Walker was still in the employ of the Loyal Land Company. He explored the western parts of Virginia for suitable settlement sites. Walker crossed southwest Virginia and passed through Cumberland Gap, which he named. The gap was already a major Indian pathway, with a well worn trail. Later the Cumberland Gap became a gateway for white settlers moving into Kentucky and the Ohio River Valley.

Shortly after Walker returned to Virginia, John Finley, a Pennsylvania trader, accompanied a Shawnee hunting party into Kentucky, where he learned about the Indian trail through Cumberland Gap. But the outbreak of the French and Indian War prevented Finley from further explorations.

DEFEAT OF THE FRENCH

After the French were defeated, the way was paved for American expansion. By 1761, hunting and trading parties regularly visited Kentucky, Tennessee and West Virginia. The mountainous portions of western North Carolina and western Virginia filled with settlers—more so after the Revolutionary War—and could no longer be considered the edge of the frontier. Growing population pressures pushed settlers beyond the mountains.

It was during duty in the French and Indian War that a North Carolinian named Daniel Boone first heard tales of the fabulous hunting beyond the mountains. In 1767, Boone made the first of several forays into Kentucky. The success of these early hunting trips enabled Boone to convince a wealthy friend, Judge Richard Henderson, to finance a major hunting and exploration expedition into the new territory. In 1769, Boone left with five other men, including John Finley, and spent two years hunting in Ken-

With the Cherokee temporarily checked, the flood of Americans into western Virginia and North Carolina turned west. Despite a British proclamation forbidding settlement beyond the crest of the Appalachians, exploratory parties began to visit Tennessee and Kentucky. Most expeditions and settlers moved west via the Valley and Ridge country of southwest Virginia, avoiding the extremely mountainous terrain in western North Carolina, and the continued threat from Cherokee villages there. Some went south into the valleys of the Watauga, Holston and Nolichucky rivers of east Tennessee, while others passed through the historic Cumberland Gap into Kentucky.

During these years, the region between the Ohio River to the north and the Tennessee River Valley to the South was uninhabited—no tribe actually lived in this region.

tucky, successfully eluding Indian hunting parties. Unfortunately for Boone, his party was attacked on its return by Cherokee Indians in the Powell River Valley of southwestern Virginia and stripped of its accumulated furs.

Not discouraged, two years later Boone, with his own and five other families, started back toward Kentucky with the intention of starting a new settlement west of the mountains. However, in the Powell River Valley the group was attacked again, this time by Shawnee Indians. The party lost several men, including Boone's eldest son, James, who was captured and tortured to death.

Another early explorer of what was then the mountainous western frontier was George Washington. As early as 1748, young Washington, then 16, worked as a surveyor in the lands west of the Shenandoah Valley. During this first expedition, he explored the headwaters of the South Branch of the Potomac in what is now West Virginia. In the next few years, Washington made several other surveying trips into the mountains of West Virginia. The skills learned in wilderness travel would prove useful later when Washington had command of the Continental forces.

Although explorers traveled the western frontier, settlers fearing Indians did not follow at once. However, in 1774, Governor of Virginia Lord Dunmore declared war on the Shawnee. They were defeated four months later at the Battle of Point Pleasant and agreed to relinquish all claims to land between the Ohio and Tennessee rivers.

Just one year after the defeat of the Shawnee, Judge Henderson, with Boone's help, signed a treaty with the Cherokees, the only other major Indian tribe with any claim to the lands west of the mountains. As part of the agreement, Henderson agreed to pay the Cherokee 10,000 pounds of goods in exchange for 20 million acres of land including the Cumberland Gap.

Even before the treaty was signed, Boone had begun to hack out a rough pathway from southwest Virginia into Kentucky. At the end of Boone's well named "Wilderness Road," the village of Boonesboro arose. Boonesboro anticipated the coming American Revolution by issuing its own Declaration of Independence on May 23, 1775.

COURTESY THE FILSON CLUB, LOUISVILLE, KY

GEORGE WUERTHNER

Above: *Fort Boonesborough in Kentucky as it looked in 1778 shortly after its establishment by Daniel Boone.*
Right: *The mountain white culture that evolved in the regions was largely self-sufficient. Wood was a natural resource used in a thousand different ways. Here a man is hand-hewing a rail fence.*

Facing page, top: *Museum of the Cherokee Indian at Cherokee, North Carolina.*
Bottom left: *The grave of Five-killer, son of Cherokee medicine woman Nancy Ward. In the early 1800s, she diligently endeavored to maintain peace between the Cherokees and the encroaching white settlers. As noted on his tombstone, Fivekiller served with U.S. forces in the War of 1812. His grave is in northwestern Georgia.*
Right: *Weaving sashes at Oconaluftee Indian Village*

58

REVOLUTIONARY WAR

When the Revolution broke out, Henderson petitioned the Continental Congress to recognize his land holdings as the 14th state. But powerful and influential Virginians such as Thomas Jefferson and Patrick Henry wished to see the region remain part of Virginia, and Henderson's request was denied. However, in recognition of his efforts to open up the West, the new states of North Carolina and Virginia granted Henderson title to more than 400,000 acres in Tennessee and Kentucky.

Daniel Boone's Wilderness Road was used during the Revolution, when George Rogers Clark led a band of Indian fighters across Kentucky to capture British forts in the Ohio River country. When the British were neutralized on the Northwest frontier, thousands of settlers poured into Kentucky—most via the Cumberland Gap. By 1783, the population had jumped to 12,000 people and, by 1800, an estimated 300,000 people had passed over this road to lands west of the mountains.

About the same time that Daniel Boone was carving out his Wilderness Road, the first permanent settlement in Tennessee was established. In 1768, several families settled on the Watauga River in east Tennessee near present-day Jonesborough. In 1775, the pioneers organized Washington County—named for George Washington—which became part of North Carolina in 1777.

During the Revolution, Indian battles persisted. The Cherokee attacked the Watauga settlements. The Indians were rebuffed, and the settlers retaliated by attacking and burning down several Cherokee villages at Chickamauga near present-day Chattanooga, Tennessee.

The American Revolution did not have a major influence on the Southern Appalachians, which was still the isolated edge of the frontier. However, mountain settlers led by John Sevier were pivotal in the defeat of Col. Patrick Ferguson at Kings Mountain. When the Articles of Confederation joined the colonies together under one central government, North Carolina ceded title to its land west of the mountains to the new federal government. Seeing an opportunity, the settlers of East Tennessee formed the new state of Franklin—named for Benjamin Franklin.

But North Carolina had second thoughts about its decision and, for four years there were two governments in eastern Tennessee, with residents split over their allegiances. Eventually, North Carolina won out and Franklin ceased to be. But after five years, in 1789, North Carolina again ceded its western lands to the federal government which promptly created the Southwest Territory. By 1795, it held enough residents for statehood, and the new state of Tennessee was admitted to the union the following year.

CHEROKEE EVICTION

As more white settlers pushed into the region, the Cherokee were continuously pushed farther and farther into the mountains. The boundaries of their reservation shrank with each new treaty, only to be lessened a few years later by yet another treaty. In 1819, the Cherokee signed their 21st treaty with the whites. Despite the concessions the Cherokee had made, when gold was discovered in northern Georgia in 1829, whites began to push for total removal of the Cherokee from their homeland.

With the election of the old Indian fighter Andrew Jackson as president, one of the more sordid chapters of American history unfolded. The U.S. government, with the full support of its highest elected official, contemptuously ignored its own agreements and began to evict the Cherokee from their homelands.

The first step in this eviction began when the Georgia legislature enacted laws to confiscate Indian lands and prohibit Indian assembly. President Jackson fully supported Georgia's actions. American citizens were guaranteed protection against seizure of property and the right of assembly by the young nation's constitution, but citizenship did not extend to Indians.

To hasten the confiscation of Indian lands, Jackson asked for, and Congress subsequently passed, a "removal law" giving the president power to force expulsion of Indians from the lands where they had resided for centuries. Davy Crockett, then a Tennessee congressman, was the

DWIGHT DYKE

AARON PASS

JOHN ELK III

59

only Tennessean to vote against the bill—and he subsequently was removed from office.

Hope glimmered briefly for the Cherokee when, in 1832, Supreme Court Justice John Marshall struck down the Georgia laws passed to restrict the rights of the Cherokee Indians. However, President Jackson refused to enforce the Supreme Court decision.

In 1835, a faction of the Cherokee tribe agreed to accept a treaty that ceded to the United States all lands east of the Mississippi in exchange for $5 million, and agreed to move westward to Indian Territory—what is today Oklahoma. Although only one tenth of the tribe endorsed the treaty, the government ratified it and ordered the removal of all Cherokee people in 1838.

The Army immediately began to round up tribal members, herding more than 17,000 Indians into stockades. In the autumn of 1838, the Indians were forced to walk westward. By the time the band reached Oklahoma, nearly 4,000 Cherokee had died from exposure, starvation and disease. The journey would be known forevermore as the "Trail of Tears."

However, despite the Army's diligent efforts to round up all the Cherokee, small groups escaped into the fastnesses of the Smoky Mountains. These people later would be allowed to stay in the East and eventually the Qualla Reservation was established for what came to be known as the Eastern Band of the Cherokee.

Most settlement had by-passed the rugged portions of the mountains, but by the late 1700s and early 1800s, not even these areas were immune from westward expansion of settlement. As early as 1795, settlers cleared land along the Oconaluftee River in what is now Great Smoky Mountains National Park. And on the opposite side of the Smokies, in what would later be Gatlinburg, Tennessee, another settlement had been established by 1802.

Farming was the basis of many of these early settlements, with individual families growing corn, oats, wheat, rye, potatoes, tobacco and fruit. A few animals, including chickens, hogs, cattle and perhaps a horse or two, were kept. Since the rugged terrain made it almost impossible to get produce to markets, most crops were grown for home consumption. Corn was frequently used to produce whiskey—an easily transportable and highly profitable source of income to mountain dwellers from the earliest times.

IRON, GOLD & COPPER

One of the earliest industries, especially in Virginia's mountains, was iron production. Stone furnaces melted the ore and separated iron from slag. Charcoal, made from wood, was the usual source of fuel, and the large demands of these early furnaces caused many acres of forest to be logged off. Iron from these furnaces was used to make cannonballs, plowshares and, with the invention of the railroad, railroad tracks.

Gold was discovered in North Carolina in 1799 and, between 1803 and 1828, the state was the only gold-producing one in the nation. Some of this gold was a by-product of copper or other mineral production. Then the discovery of gold at Dahlonega, Georgia in 1828 set off a major rush to that area.

Copper also was mined in the Southern Appalachians. The largest mines were in the Ducktown area near the junction of the Georgia, Tennessee and North Carolina borders. First discovered in 1847, copper from these mines was critical to the South during the Civil War, as more than 90 percent of the Confederacy's copper came from this one location. Years of mining and smelting left the hills surrounding Ducktown denuded of vegetation, like a landscape of the Southwest canyon country.

Despite the sporadic spurts of industrial development here and there, for the most part the mountains remained relatively isolated and outside the mainstream of American development as the frontier moved westward. However, some events penetrated even the mountain fastnesses.

ANOTHER STATE IS BORN

Few mountaineers could have been considered supportive of slavery. Poor and independent themselves, they had no use for preserving the institution. Perhaps not so surprisingly, a good number of Southern Appalachian resi-

ABOVE: GEORGE WUERTHNER; LEFT: AARON PASS

Above: *Dahlonega Courthouse, Georgia, built in 1836. The area was the site of an 1829 gold rush.*
Left: *Gold still can be found, in small quantities, in western North Carolina and northern Georgia.*
Facing page: *Catherine Iron Furnace, Massanutten Mountain, Virginia. Iron production was one of the region's earliest industries.*

61

Above: *Brotherton Cabin, Chicka-mauga National Military Park, Georgia. The battle of Chickamauga was one of the critical engagements of the Civil War, allowing Union soldiers to move from west of the Tennessee mountains into Georgia.*
Facing page: *Mill at Pigeon Forge, Tennessee. The many rivers rising in the Appalachians provided water power crucial to the South's early industrial development.*

ginia. Largely pro-Union, the mountainous part of what was then Virginia opposed secession from the Union. After Virginia voted to join the Confederacy, a group of western-ers set up a pro-union state government in Wheeling. For a while, Virginia had two state governments—one in Wheel-ing and another in Richmond, each claiming authority for the entire state.

Eventually a West Virginia statehood convention was held in Wheeling, where delegates adopted an abolition platform and voted to join the Union. The U.S. Congress accepted West Virginia, and President Lincoln signed the law making it the 35th state.

A MOUNTAIN BARRIER IN THE CIVIL WAR

During the Civil War, military actions occurred around the perimeter of the Southern Appalachians, but no major battles actually were fought in the mountains. However, bloody skirmishes and raids did occur in the highlands and, perhaps more importantly, the war brought about bitter di-visions among families and communities that lasted for de-cades. The mountain barrier split the war zone into two major theaters—the eastern seaboard and the western fron-tier. More battles were fought in Tennessee in the western theater than in any other state besides Virginia.

One of the war's more important battles occurred on the southern fringe of the Southern Appalachian region, at Chickamauga Creek south of Chattanooga, Tennessee. Here, through a gap in the mountains, a railroad line ran from Atlanta into Tennessee. Capture of the Chattanooga area would mean controlling movement between the Mis-sissippi drainage, occupied by Union forces, and the coast—under Confederate control. The intensity of the battle on September 19-20, 1863, hints at the relative im-portance of this strategic location. In this one battle, more than 32,000 men from both sides were killed, wounded or reported missing. The battle of Chickamauga was pivotal since it paved the way for the eventual fall and capture by Union troops of Atlanta, one of the South's major rail and industrial centers.

Up in the northern end of the Southern Appalachians

dents sided with the Union. East Tennessee, for example, sent more troops to the Federal forces than to the Confed-erate side. Many mountain villages remained loyal to the Union, sometimes to the point that Confederate sympa-thizers risked their lives if they openly supported the south-ern position. For instance, the residents of White Oak Flats, now Gatlinburg, beat up a particularly vocal Confed-erate supporter, who eventually was forced to leave town.

The Civil War also led to the creation of West Vir-

another area saw Civil War action. A number of battles took place in the Shenandoah Valley, where Confederate General Stonewall Jackson outmaneuvered Union troops on numerous occasions. Jackson's presence occupied northern troops who sought to defend Washington, D.C., which was less than a hundred miles way, and also kept them from engaging in battles elsewhere.

Stonewall Jackson's presence in the Shenandoah Valley kept this fertile breadbasket in Confederate hands. Many historians believe that if the Union had occupied and devastated just this one valley, they might have brought the South to its knees much sooner. However, the Union did not turn to such brutal tactics to break the fighting ability of the South until Sherman's march to the sea in Georgia, where everything in a 60-mile swath was burned or looted.

After the war, railroads began to penetrate the mountains. Beginning in the 1870s and continuing into the 1880s, railroads were built throughout the mountain uplands. They had a profound impact, ending much of the region's cultural isolation and facilitating large-scale industrial resource exploitation. The railroads also enabled the tourist and health resort industries to begin.

LIFESTYLE OF THE HIGHLANDERS

Much has been written about the mountaineer, highlander or hillbilly, as the poor mountain folks were known. Big families were the rule, with 10 or 12 children the usual brood. A report on the mountain people of Kentucky written in 1901 paints a vivid picture of the limited world some highlanders experienced: "We met one woman who, during the twelve years of her married life, had lived only ten miles across the mountain from her own home, but had never in this time been back home to visit her father and mother. Another in Perry county told me she had never been farther from home than Hazard, the county-seat, which is only six miles distant. Another had never been to the post office, four miles away!"

Farming was the main occupation and corn the main crop. On the steep slopes, erosion was rampant, and after a

few years, the soil would be worn out and the family would have to clear a new field or move to a new location. Stories are told about the steep areas under cultivation. A common joke was about the farmer who fell out of his corn field and broke his neck.

Mountaineers raised small numbers of livestock— mostly cattle and hogs. Hogs roamed the woods freely feeding on nuts and roots, while cattle often were taken up to the grassy balds where a lone keeper might tend them all summer.

Church life was important for spiritual reasons, and also was the focus for social events. Baptist, Methodist and Presbyterian were the most common denominations.

Given the isolated nature of the mountain communities, it was not unusual for close kin relationships to exist between residents. Fighting and violence between family groups sometimes lasted for decades, and one of the most famous was the Hatfield-McCoy feud. The Hatfields lived in West Virginia while the McCoys resided just across the state line in Kentucky. What started the feud has long been lost to romantic conjecture; however, the first casualty occurred in 1882 when a Hatfield was shot during a disagreement with several McCoys. Three McCoys were arrested, but a gang of Hatfields kidnapped the trio while they were being transported to a jail and killed them. The feud ran into the 1920s, with Hatfields killing McCoys on sight and always being acquitted by West Virginia juries composed entirely of Hatfields or their sympathizers, while McCoys who killed Hatfields enjoyed similar immunity in Kentucky courts. Finally, in 1921, federal troops were sent in to stop the shootings.

The Southern Appalachians mountaineers were famous for their whiskey-making. Nearly every hill farmer grew corn, and some of them made whiskey of what was not consumed as food by family or animals. Given the rough or nonexistent roads, getting farm produce to market was nearly impossible. Whatever went out of the mountains was more than likely carried on a person's back or by packhorse. Items sold in distant markets had to be small, light and highly transportable—as well as valuable enough

to make the effort worthwhile. Whiskey filled these requirements.

Shortly after the United States was formed, Alexander Hamilton proposed levying a tax on whiskey. The tax generated the Whiskey Rebellion among frontier farmers in western Pennsylvania who perceived that one of their few income-producing products was being unfairly taxed. President George Washington ordered federal troops to quell the revolt.

Illegal whiskey production continued, and gradually acquired a certain respectability among the mountaineers. To make moonshine whiskey was seen as more an act of independence than a crime, and almost every backwoodsman had a still hidden among the laurels and coves. In 1876 the Commissioner of Internal Revenue wrote:

"I can safely say that during the past year not less than 3,000 illicit stills have been operated in the districts named [Southern Appalachians]. Those stills are of a producing capacity of 10 to 15 gallons a day. They are usually located at inaccessible points in the mountains, away from the ordinary lines of travel, and are generally owned by unlettered men of desperate character, armed and ready to resist the officers of the law....and when arrests are made it often occurs that prisoners are rescued by mob violence, and officers and witnesses are often dragged from their homes and cruelly beaten, or waylaid and assassinated."

Revenue collectors, the commissioner noted, were seen by the mountain people as "emissaries from some foreign country quartered upon the people for the collection of tribute."

Moonshine whiskey avoided the government tax, hence was cheaper than liquor produced in distilleries. With the coming of prohibition, the value of moonshine rose to new heights and so did the amount of backwoods production. The profit per gallon went from about a dollar to three to six dollars or more—a large sum of money for the rural population.

With the coming of the automobile, illicit whiskey found a much larger market. "Blockaders" with specially built cars tried to elude government agents. The cars, often

Facing page: Methodist church at Cades Cove, Great Smoky Mountains National Park. In the isolated mountain communities, churches functioned not only as religious centers, but also as social centers.

looking old and well used, had hidden tanks to carry whiskey, and they had racing car engines, suspensions and brakes.

TIMBERING AND MILL TOWNS

The isolation of the mountain people was disrupted around the turn of the century when industrial logging came to the region. The mountaineers had, of course, cut timber before. Trees were cleared for farms, for use in the manufacture of charcoal, for mining smelters and for lumber. However, nothing done previously matched the changes that occurred just after the turn of the 20th century.

Big timber companies who already had stripped the forests of New England, the Adirondacks, and the Lakes States now turned their eyes to the virgin hardwood forests of the Southern Appalachians. A report on area forests submitted to President Theodore Roosevelt concluded that these were the "heaviest and most beautiful hardwood forests of the continent." Such glowing reports could not fail to attract the interest of the timber barons. At that time the southern mountains held no federal lands and everything was under private ownership. The timber companies moved in and bought huge tracts of land. Champion Coated Paper Company, for example, bought 90,000 acres within what is now Great Smoky Mountains National Park.

In the days before the chain saw and skidder, turning forests into lumber was not an easy task. First, trees had to be cut laboriously with axes and cross-cut saws. Oxen or horses skidded the logs to landings. Sometimes loggers built flumes, or wooden aqueducts, to carry logs down a mountain. At some strategic point, logs were gathered and then loaded onto trains pulled by short, powerful locomotives that could climb very steep grades. The old railroad grades are still visible in many parts of the Southern Appalachians, and today often are used as hiking trails.

Mill towns and logging camps sprang up in remote parts of the mountains. Places like Elkmont and Smokemont, now in Great Smoky Mountains National Park, once were bustling communities. The new-found cash brought a

TOP: GLENN VAN NIMWEGEN

LEFT: GEORGE WUERTHNER

certain prosperity, and many a mountaineer found a job skidding logs, cutting timber or working in a mill. But the boom was short-lived. Most companies were not in for the long haul; they were timber mining. The Little River Lumber Company alone cut more than 2 billion board feet of timber from the region. To make a comparison, that is more than twice the timber cut annually by *all* companies operating on national forest lands in Montana and Idaho today. Once the forests were cleared, the companies packed up their saws and mills, put them on railroad cars and headed west to the great old-growth timber of the Pacific Northwest.

Fire often accompanied logging operations. Slash left on denuded hillsides became tinder-dry. Sparks from railroad trains and careless individuals started more than one fire that left behind a wasteland.

NATIONAL FORESTS AND NATIONAL PARKS

The sight of ravaged landscapes and denuded hills, along with the resultant floods and severe erosion, spawned a new conservation movement in the Southern Appalachians. Early in this century, the federal government began to buy huge tracts of land to establish national forests in the eastern United States. Unlike western national forests, most of which were carved from existing federally owned public domain, the eastern forests had to be purchased. In 1911 the passage of the Weeks Act allowed the federal government to buy lands within specific boundaries for new national forests. It was during this era that forests like the Cherokee, Pisgah and Jefferson were established.

In addition to the creation of new national forests, there was a growing recognition that some of the Southern Appalachians should be preserved as a national park. Various areas were studied and proposed for potential national park status, including the Mt. Mitchell area of the Black Range in North Carolina, the Blue Ridge adjacent to the Shenandoah Valley, and the Great Smoky Mountains straddling the border of Tennessee and North Carolina.

At the turn of the century, an Appalachian National Park Association sprang up in Asheville, North Carolina.

The group proposed that a national park be established somewhere in the region, but there was not enough federal support at the time for the proposal to succeed.

By the 1920s, the mood in Washington had changed and Congress was receptive to the idea of a national park in the Appalachians. A quiet librarian turned mountain explorer, Horace Kephart, lobbied for a national park in the Great Smoky Mountains. Kephart came to the mountains looking for adventure and to improve his health, and he achieved both. He also fell in love with the Smoky Mountains and did not want to see any further logging of the remaining virgin forests. Kephart, author of several books including *Our Southern Highlanders*, plus numerous magazine articles, began to publicize the park concept.

A Great Smoky Mountains National Park Association was formed and with the blessings of the Department of Interior, money was raised and lands in both Tennessee and North Carolina purchased to establish the new park. Great Smoky Mountains National Park was dedicated in 1940, and today it has the largest visitation of any national park in the country.

A similar citizen movement helped create Shenandoah National Park in Virginia. Lands were purchased and in 1936 the new park was officially opened. Anchored by a national park on each end, the Blue Ridge Parkway was built as a scenic roadway connection.

These national parks, national forests and other scenic attractions have proven to be a major impetus for most of the recent economic growth in and around the region. As the Southern Appalachian region faces the 21st century, the main problem will be coping with growth, while preserving the proverbial goose that lays the golden egg.

National parks and national forests have been a major impetus for economic growth around the region.

Facing page, top: Memories of farm life in the Cable Mill area at Cades Cove.
Bottom: Around the turn of the 20th century, lumber companies moved into the Southern Appalachians buying huge parcels of land and timbering off the region's magnificent forests. Little River Lumber Company Museum, Tennessee.

6

GREAT SMOKY MOUNTAINS NATIONAL PARK

Above: *Wild geraniums in Great Smoky Mountains National Park.*

Facing page: *A hazy sunrise just below Newfound Gap in the park.*

The best known and most celebrated portion of the Southern Appalachians lies within the bounds of 517,000-acre Great Smoky Mountains National Park on the North Carolina-Tennessee border. The Great Smokies contain some of the highest peaks on the Eastern Seaboard, and represent one of the most important biological preserves in the entire Southern Appalachian bioregion. For this reason, the park has been designated an International Biosphere Preserve—under a program that registers globally significant, representative ecosystems.

REVERTED TO WOODLANDS

Despite the fact that much of the land that now makes up the park once was logged or farmed, most of it except for agricultural areas like Cades Cove has reverted to woodlands. Many parts of the now-forested park—such as the area surrounding Sugarlands Visitor Center and The Chimneys Picnic area—were once corn fields.

But the greatest treasure of the Smokies is the more than 40 percent of the park that is still virgin woodlands—the largest tract of unlogged forest on the entire Eastern Seaboard. Only recently did scientists realize the complexity and diversity found in such unmanaged old-growth landscapes. And the Smokies are the only sizable preserve where stands of virgin timber can be studied and compared with managed timberlands and manipulated landscape that dominate beyond the park borders.

The virgin forests of the Southern Appalachian Mountains are among the most diverse in the temperate region of the world. Some of the best examples of these biologically complex woodlands are within the Smokies. An elevational range between 850 feet and 6,600 feet, combined with annual precipitation of more than 85 inches, has created an amazing diversity of micro-habitats. In addition, since the Smokies were too far south to support glaciers during past Ice Ages, they were a refugium for many species driven south during those colder periods. As a consequence of these and other factors, the Smokies boast more than 100 tree species. In comparison, in the whole state of Alaska, an area more than 700 times greater than Great Smoky Mountains National Park, there are only 33 species of trees.

The Smokies' incredible diversity of trees includes five species of maple, five species of hickory, six species of pine and three native species of magnolia. Some species relatively rare elsewhere are abundant here. For instance, 75 percent of the world's population of Fraser fir, a major component of the high-elevation spruce-fir zone, occurs within the bounds of the park. On the other hand, there are some rarities as well—the southernmost known specimen of mountain paper birch, a species common in New England, is found here.

Some of these trees reach immense proportions. Yellow poplar, or tulip tree, may grow to be 150 feet tall and have a circumferance of 23 feet! Large specimens of white pine, eastern hemlock, basswood and other trees can be found in the old-growth forests of the park.

Sadly, the American chestnut, which once made up 50 percent of these forests and attained huge dimensions, is nearly extinct. A fungus, introduced from China into the United States in 1904, ravaged chestnuts throughout its natural range. Today, the chestnut survives, sprouting from its original roots, but as soon as the trees achieve a diameter

Above: *Autumn palette in the Oconaluftee River Valley.*

Facing page: *On the West Prong, Little Pigeon River tributary.*

of three to six inches, the fungus kills the above-ground bole. One can glean a sense of the majesty of these trees because the rot-resistant wood decays slowly. In a few parts of the park, chestnut logs still rest on the ground (for instance, in the Roaring Fork drainage). Another exotic disease, dogwood anthracnose, threatens one of the park's most beautiful symbols—flowering dogwood.

BIOLOGICAL DIVERSITY

But trees are only a part of the Smokies' incredible biodiversity. Biologists have recorded more than 2,000 species of fungi, and 1,568 species of flowering plants. Bird watchers may glimpse one of 200 bird species, while 50 types of mammals roam the woods of the Smokies. Perhaps due to the overall mild climate, reptiles and amphibians are well represented with more than 80 species, while 22 different kinds of salamanders are recorded for the park—including the endemic red-cheeked salamander, found nowhere else

on earth. Even the park's fish populations are amazingly diverse, with more than 70 species of freshwater fish recorded here.

Biologists continue to add species to the list known for the park. As recently as 1988, 15 plants previously unrecorded in the park were discovered. The northern flying squirrel, a threatened and endangered species in the Southern Appalachians, was rediscovered after a 50-year absence.

Preservation of this biological diversity is increasingly recognized as one of the most important values of our public lands system. Yet, despite its protected status, many species have already been extirpated from the park. The Pigeon River takes its name from the now extinct passenger pigeon. Bison were known to graze the balds on the crest of the Smokies, and their trails were often the first pathways people followed through the wilderness. Elk, too, were known to exist, hence the name Elkmont within the park. Feeding on these prey animals were predators like wolves and mountain lions.

While the passenger pigeon never will be brought back, other extirpated species may someday roam these mountains again. River otters recently were reintroduced into the park and appear to be doing well. There is no biological reason why bison, rather than cattle, should not graze Cades Cove, and elk once again could be seen at Elkmont. If these animals were successfully returned to the park, then predators like wolves and mountain lions could once again roam these hills as well.

Other native species are not yet extinct, but are nevertheless in trouble. Brook trout, the only native trout in the park, has been declining. The Smokies brook trout is genetically distinct from brook trout in New England. Restocking the Smokies with trout from elsewhere is not a desirable alternative to saving the present populations.

One factor contributing to the decline of this native fish is the introduction of non-native trout, in particular the rainbow trout. The rainbow outcompetes the brookies for both food and space. In many streams, the brook trout have been pushed into the less desirable habitat and frequently survive only in the smallest headwaters where the rainbow do not go or in upper sections of waterways where waterfalls prevent the upstream passage of rainbows.

The wild boar also causes problems in the park. It was brought to North Carolina from Europe and placed on a private game preserve in 1912. In the early 1920s, about a hundred of these animals escaped and subsequently dispersed into the mountains. By the 1940s, wild boars were reported in the southwest corner of the park by Calderwood and, since then, the animals have gradually expanded their range eastward. They are most common in the region west of Newfound Gap. No one knows how many boars are in the park, but estimates place their population between 500 and 2,000 animals.

Boars tear up the ground in their search for food, eating the tubers of many native wildflowers. Their persistence in foraging for these flowers may wipe out many native plant species. In the fall, they consume large amounts of acorns, and in years of poor mast production, may deprive native wildlife of this rich food source. In addition, they eat small vertebrates like the red-cheeked salamander.

The Park Service is trying to eradicate these pigs. However, the dense vegetation makes control difficult and expensive. Furthermore, pigs have very high reproductive capacities, since each female can bear four to eight piglets twice a year.

Devising a publicly acceptable control method has been difficult. The most effective means identified so far is shooting the animals. Even this is expensive and time consuming for the limited park staff available.

Not everyone is happy with this method. Hunters in both Tennessee and North Carolina like to hunt boars. Hunters also claim that killing wild boars by park personnel is a waste of meat. However, the dead animals are recycled in the ecosystem and provide food for carrion eaters, enriching the forest that produced them.

Other members of the public do not like the idea that anyone kills these exotic animals. However, one of the main purposes of our national park system is the preservation of natural biodiversity and the exotic wild boar threatens native plant and animal communities. No matter what

GEORGE WUERTHNER

kind of control is implemented, it will probably always have to be in effect, since wild boar are actually stocked on public and private lands outside the park in order to provide increased opportunities for hunters.

PEOPLE ON THE LAND

Besides being a biological preserve, the Great Smoky Mountains National Park also preserves a part of America's historical roots. At Mingus Mill, Oconaluftee, Cades Cove, Roaring Fork and Cataloochee, the National Park Service has restored and maintained cabins, churches, schools and other buildings from early white settlements. However, the earliest known human settlement in the region was not white, but Indian.

The Cherokee Indians invaded the Southern Appalachians sometime after 1000 A.D. By the time the first Europeans explored the region in the mid-1500s, the Cherokee had well established villages surrounding the Smokies, with communities located on the Tennessee River in Tennessee and on the French Broad River in North Carolina.

Beginning in 1795, notwithstanding that the Cherokee lived in the surrounding valleys, the first whites settled the North Carolina side of what would later be Great Smoky Mountains National Park. By 1800, settlers moved into the Tennessee side of the mountains as well, and as early as 1802, the first white child, Daniel Reagan, was born in White Oak, later called Gatlinburg.

As the lower valleys filled up, people moved higher into the mountains. Cades Cove, a mountain-rimmed valley, was settled by John Oliver in 1819. Other mountain valleys in the Smokies including Cataloochee, Sugarlands and Roaring Fork soon had their own settlements. By 1850, Cades Cove had more than 600 people, and residents of Cataloochee once numbered 700.

For the most part, these communities were more or less self-sufficient. Each family grew corn, vegetables and fruits, and had a few chickens and cattle. Hunting and fishing supplied additional fresh meat.

For almost a hundred years, life more or less followed this general pattern. Then, around the turn of the century,

GEORGE WUERTHNER

DWIGHT DYKE

Above: *Dogwood, one of the Smokies' distinctive spring flowering shrubs, soon may disappear due to an exotic introduced disease that is ravaging the tree throughout the country.*
Left: *The brilliance of rhododendrons adds to the Great Smoky Mountains' beauty.*

Facing page: *Little Pigeon River by The Chimneys area.*

73

Above: *John Oliver's cabin at Cades Cove.*
Right: *Red salamander, one of 22 salamander species that live in the park.*

Facing page: *Flame azalea adorns Gregory Bald.*

FREDERICK D. ATWOOD

big-time logging came to the Southern Appalachians. In 1901, the Little River Timber Company bought 85,000 acres in Tennessee's Little River drainage. Champion Paper Company bought 90,000 acres on the North Carolina side of the divide in the Deep Creek and Oconaluftee River drainages. Towns soon sprang up in the woods—Elkmont, Smokemont and Fontana were all logging camps—and many mountaineers went to work in the woods. Railroads built to these camps ended much of the isolation that had dominated many of the mountain communities. Later, railroad beds became roads—the present road along the Little River between Townsend and Elkmont was originally the bed of a logging railroad.

As elsewhere in the region, land here was devastated by logging. Flumes (including one on Clingmans Dome) and trails for moving cut timber scarred the land, and sparks from the trains set slash fires. By the 1920s, the giant forests of the Smokies were in ruins when a movement began to create a national park here. This meant buying the privately-owned farms and timberlands.

The park initiative began in 1923, led by a citizen's group known as the Great Smoky Mountains Conservation Association. At this time, more than 6,000 separate private holdings lay within the bounds of the proposed park. Most of the acreage was held by timber companies, but more than 5,000 small parcels, including farms and summer home sites, were located within the purchase area as well.

Although not all these land owners were supportive of the park buy-out, many did not oppose it. Most of the timber companies were willing to sell—for a high enough price. Many of the mountain farmers were ready to take the money and start a new life elsewhere.

By 1926, the Conservation Association had successfully raised more than a million dollars and the legislatures of both North Carolina and Tennessee soon contributed more than $2 million to the cause. John D. Rockefeller, Jr., one of the major donors, contributed another $5 million. The states of Tennessee and North Carolina set up special park commissions to supervise land acquisitions, and eventually donated these holdings to the federal government.

Today, the park is a major tourist attraction and receives the heaviest visitation of any national park in the U.S. Recently, as many as 10 million visitors have come in a single year. While summer is busy, fall weekends get the largest crowds when people come to view the autumn color.

The park has a number of scenic drives, including the loop roads around Roaring Fork and Cades Cove, as well as the Newfound Gap road that crosses the range. But the best way to see the park is by hiking. There are more than 900 miles of trail, including 70 miles of the Appalachian Trail. While one could spend a week or more on the trails, many of the park trails are relatively short and enjoyable as afternoon strolls, rather than major treks.

The Smokies are the single largest intact wildlands in the Southern Appalachians. Several bills introduced in Congress would designate much of the Smokies back country as protected wilderness, which would prohibit any development, roads or other unnatural disturbance.

PRESERVING GEOLOGICAL HISTORY

The Great Smoky Mountains are a microcosm of the geological history of the Southern Appalachians. Resting on the ancient eastern edge of the North American continental plate, the rocks found within the Smokies are, not surprisingly, rather old—between a billion years and 350 million years in age. By contrast, the oldest rocks in Oregon on the younger western edge of the continent are approximately 200 million years old.

Straddling the dividing line between two major physiographic divisions, the Smokies represent the transition from the older metamorphic rocks of the Blue Ridge and the younger sedimentary rocks of the Valley and Ridge province. The oldest rocks, more than a billion years in age, are Precambrian metamorphic rocks. These ancient rocks have been changed by heat and pressure into more or less uniform, very hard rock, such as granite and gneiss. These rocks are confined to the eastern edge of the park in North Carolina. Bryson City, Cherokee and the Raven Fork River are all underlain by these ancient rocks.

Above: Violets in Roaring Fork Valley are among the park's 1,500 species of wildflowers.

Facing page: Preservation of the Southern Appalachian cultural heritage is one of the park's missions. Here at Pioneer Village, a replica of a mountain settlement.

The vast bulk of rocks in the park are metamorphosed sedimentary rocks a billion to 500 million years old, including schists, quartzites, shales, slates and sandstones. Depending on the degree of metamorphism, these sedimentary rocks are recognizable by their layering, which also may be dipped on an angle. One of these rock formations, the Thunderhead Sandstones, makes up the crest of the Smokies as well as many of the ledges in quite a few of the waterfalls on the Tennessee side of the park. Laurel Falls, Ramsey Cascades, and the Sinks all flow over erosion-resistant beds of Thunderhead Sandstones.

In a few areas of Valley and Ridge province structures, erosion of older overlying rocks exposes the younger rocks beneath, in what geologists call "windows." These geological windows form prominent mountain valleys called coves, such as Tuckaleechee, Wears and Cades Cove. Since the underlying limestones exposed in these windows weathered to deep, fertile soils, these coves were attractive areas for farming.

Erosion-resistant sandstones make up much of the Smokies' crest. For 36 miles, this divide reaches more than 4,900 feet above sea level; 16 peaks are above 6,000 feet. Despite the great height of these peaks, they are sandwiched between two major rivers—the Big Pigeon River on the north and the Little Tennessee on the south. Since rivers do not usually cut through mountain ranges, this reveals relative age: The general course of these rivers predated the uplift of the Smokies.

But not all the rivers are that ancient. Some, such as the Oconaluftee River, begin on the Smokies' crest. Many such streams follow fault lines. The occurrence of major river valleys, the way the land leaps up from Gatlinburg to Mt. LeConte, and prominent ridges like Chilhowee Mountain, are all the result of faulting. Faults are actual breaks or fractures in the earth's crust where one segment of crust has moved. A sudden movement is felt as an earthquake.

It is not surprising that rivers often follow these crustal breaks. The nearly linear path of the Oconaluftee River, as seen from Newfound Gap, marks the Oconaluftee Fault. The Greenbrier Fault marks the western slope of the Smokies and is notable as the natural change in slope marked by Mt. LeConte above Gatlinburg. The Great Smoky Fault is marked by the abrupt rise of Chilhowee Mountain.

THE PARK'S FUTURE

As Great Smoky Mountains National Park approaches the 21st century, it is in many ways in better condition than when it was established. The forest cover has grown back. Wildlife then nearly extinct—like the black bear—are numerous again, and other species extirpated—like the river otter—are being reintroduced.

However, the Great Smokies suffer too from the demands of a modern world. Acid rainfall is killing the forests. Smog obscures the views. Roads, trails and campgrounds often are crowded. The surrounding private lands are being developed, gradually eating away at buffers that existed around the park. Exotic diseases like the chestnut blight and animals like the wild boar threaten native species.

Despite these problems, Great Smokies is a world-class natural preserve and a source of both regional and national pride. It is a park that ranks with the best in our nation and, with care and luck, it will remain that way into the future.

7 IN THE FUTURE

Rapid change is coming to the Southern Appalachians. Interstate highways have put the region within a day's drive of nearly half the U.S. population. As our society ages, more and more people seek out the small, quiet towns for retirement. While the birth rate for the Southern Appalachians has remained relatively flat, the number of immigrants has jumped dramatically. Not all these newcomers are retirees. The expanding economy of the region attracts new workers as well.

Western North Carolina is representative of this expanded population growth. Between 1970 and 1980, the population here grew by an average of 25 percent. Macon County grew 47 percent, while Henderson County doubled its population from 1960 to 1987.

In 1989, the North Carolina legislature passed an $8.8 billion highway bill to "put 95 percent of the residents of the state within 10 miles of a four-lane road." Improved access will undoubtedly bring more people. And while such a boom might boost business for developers and real estate brokers, it is not necessarily a positive trend for local residents. More people means higher taxes to pay for improved infrastructure—schools, highways, and waste disposal services. Also likely are more crime, more congestion, water and air pollution.

Above: *The Southern Appalachians are the outdoor playground for the southeast. Here a kayaker challenges the Ocoee River, Tennessee.*

Facing page: *View from Rocky Knob on the Blue Ridge Parkway, Virginia.*

A HOST OF CONCERNS

New highways also potentially fragment wildlife habitat. Studies by black bear specialist Dr. Michael Pelton show that heavy traffic on a four-lane can pose a major barrier to wildlife movements. Wildlife restricted into smaller islands face problems with genetic isolation and inbreeding.

A growing problem throughout the Southern Appalachians is garbage disposal. According to one estimate, a third of North Carolina's landfills will run out of space by 1993. Of the western mountain counties, 10 out of 17 will run out of space within the next five years.

In rural areas, there are few regulations on building and construction. Many homes are built with inadequate or leaky septic systems. Ground pollution is already a problem and is getting worse. But the problem is not necessarily confined to the rural areas. Asheville's sewage system is old and overworked. Cracked sewage lines near the French Broad River allow sewer and river water to mix. In addition the cracked lines increase the flow of sewage into the sewage treatment plant after heavy rains—sometimes as much as 10 times normal flows. Whenever this happens a bypass valve allows raw sewage to flow directly into the river. Expanding the present sewage treatment plant and repairing the old pipes will be costly and take years.

Groundwater pollution threatens a region that has traditionally had very high-quality water sources. Many residents depend directly upon ground water for their drinking water. North Carolina, for instance, ranks second in the nation in terms of the number of households that rely upon groundwater for their drinking supplies.

Air pollution is regional as well as national problem, even in near-wilderness settings. For instance, although Great Smoky Mountains National Park is a designated Class 1 area—the most stringent classification under the

GEORGE WUERTHNER

On Hickory Creek, Madison County, North Carolina.

Clean Air Act—pollution from industrial sources outside the park, as well as automobile use in the park, compromise this status.

Only four to 10 percent of the haze that gave the Smokies their name comes from natural sources. The haze is now whitish, composed primarily of acid sulfates produced by coal-fired power generation plants and other industrial sources west of the park. Pollution from places like Houston, Birmingham, the Ohio River Valley and other industrial areas can arrive in the Southern Appalachians within 24 hours. The present practice of allowing pollution sources to build higher smokestacks, rather than limiting and regulating what comes out of the stack, contributes to this problem by dispersing pollutants over a larger area.

When combined with water, these sulfates produce acid rain, which is responsible for a decline in the vigor and health of Southern Appalachian forests. Some attribute the wide-spread death of high-elevation red spruce to acid rain and accompanying atmospheric deposition.

Local pollution sources are a problem as well. Many mountain valleys suffer from inversions as cool air settles to the ground, creating stagnant air and trapping pollution. This pollution comes from a variety of sources, such as wood stoves and local industries like the large Champion Pulp Mill in Canton, North Carolina.

Many of these environmental concerns can be dealt with by careful planning and adequate regulation. However, whether people of the Southern Appalachians are willing to forgo some economic opportunities to maintain a healthy environment and a high quality of life remains to be seen. A local resident of Highlands, North Carolina said in response to the question of growth: "People talk about the good old days. I grew up in the good old days and I don't want to go back to them when you couldn't make a living."

INCREASINGLY DESIRABLE

Undoubtedly, there is no going back. The Southern Appalachians are increasingly seen as a very desirable place to live. Asheville, North Carolina was selected by Rand McNally's *Places Rated Almanac* in the late 1980s as "the best place to live in America" for metropolitan areas under 250,000. Quality of life is increasingly recognized as a major contributor to economic growth as well as tourism.

And the contribution of tourism is substantial. Tourism generated an estimated $840 million in western North Carolina alone in 1988, and it has been growing at a rate of better than nine percent per year. Projections make it the growth industry of the world in the 1990s, and nowhere is this more apparent than in the Southern Appalachians, where millions visit annually.

The Nantahala and Pisgah national forests alone get more visitors than the top 10 national parks. More than 25 million people visited the Blue Ridge Parkway in western North Carolina. Annual visitation at Great Smoky Mountains National Park topped 10 million people in 1987.

There is no reason to believe that this trend will not continue. At current rates of increase, in 20 years visitors to the Blue Ridge Parkway will number 46 million per year! Depending upon how the region manages this anticipated deluge of people, the future can be either manageable or an economic and environmental disaster.

Tourism brings its own problems, and in this region depends upon maintaining a high-quality environment with beautiful scenery, clean water and uncrowded woodlands. The Southern Appalachian national forests figure prominently in any discussion of tourism and recreation since they constitute the vast majority of public lands in the entire region.

MANAGEMENT DISCUSSIONS

For this reason, the issue of how to manage these lands has become a regional and national issue. In particular, the issue of timber harvest on public lands has come under increasing fire and scrutiny. In terms of timber supply the national forests of the Southern Appalachians provide a tiny percentage of the timber cut within the southeast—most timber comes from private lands which tend to be more accessible, more productive, and have overall gentler terrain. And, while timber harvest from national forest lands doubled during the years 1977-1986, the price paid for trees cut declined, because public lands tend to be less accessible—making the cost of harvest higher.

Environmentalists argue that the below-cost timber sales do not represent the real costs to the public. Taxpayer subsidization of timber harvest is more than the cost of road building and sale administration, because clearcutting impacts water quality, scenery, wildlife habitat and biodiversity.

Despite the relative unimportance of national forest timber as a source of logs for the timber industry, environmentalists claim the priorities of the Forest Service are skewed towards timber harvest. For instance, more than 40 percent of the Nantahala-Pisgah National Forest budget is allocated to timber harvest and road building, while only 3.4 percent is devoted to wildlife. All the national forests

FREDERICK D. ATWOOD

GEORGE WUERTHNER

Above: As more people flock to the Southern Appalachians for retirement or second homes, suburban development increasingly encroaches upon farmland.
Left: Timber production is important in the Southeast, but comparatively little timber is cut in the mountains. By far the best uses of these mountain timberlands are watershed protection, recreation and preservation of biological diversity.

in the Southern Appalachians have called for expanded timber harvest in the coming decades.

Part of the environmentalists' concern centers on clearcutting, in which all the trees are stripped from a particular site. The resulting patchwork of open holes in an otherwise solid canopy of forest is visually disturbing, but has ecological ramifications as well. For instance, forest-interior–dwelling songbirds are very vulnerable to predation as well as nest parasitism when mature closed forest canopy is eliminated. The resulting fragmentation and greater access created by roads threatens a host of wildlife species from black bear to northern flying squirrel. Yet, nearly every national forest plan recommended not only increased timber harvest, but also the use of clearcutting as the predominant means of timber harvest.

The Forest Service justifies increased timber harvest by claiming that biodiversity is increased by breaking up the forest, creating more edge effect and thus more potential habitat for wildlife. However, biologists counter that the Forest Service focus is too narrow. If viewed from a regional perspective, including private lands with housing developments, highways, logging and agriculture, there is already an abundance of edge effect. What is rare, they claim, is older, mature forest and large patches of undisturbed wildlife habitat. In fact, the only places where these values can be found or preserved are on federal lands.

Environmentalists believe that the best use of these public lands is for preservation of scenic qualities, watershed protection, wildlife and wilderness values, as well as recreation opportunities. They argue the Forest Service should make protection of these values the highest priority, with timber harvest practiced only where it can be demonstrated to enhance the other values.

The Forest Service is reevaluating its forest plans and there is reason to believe that the agency will place ever-increasing emphasis upon wildlife, recreation, wildlands and scenic values.

But changing the emphasis from logging to recreation or wildlife will not be completely successful without additional coordination between various agencies as well as

among the different national forests. Under impetus provided by the Man and Biosphere program, a Greater Smoky Mountains Ecosystem concept is being developed which would provide coordinated management for lands within the Great Smoky Mountains National Park as well as surrounding national forest lands.

The Southern Appalachians are a national treasure worthy of national attention and national pride. As one of the major centers of biological diversity—with a wealth of scenic, watershed and wildlife attributes that are globally significant—the Southern Appalachians are truly one of America's crown jewels. Increasingly, people of the region call for restoration of the landscape: regenerate the cathedral-like old growth hardwood forests, keep the waters clean, repair the damage from 200 years of neglect and abuse, and preserve the biological and cultural attributes of this unique region.

The Southern Appalachians are at a crossroads in changing land use, land values and social values. How well the transformation is made to a "kinder, gentler" relationship with the earth will test our knowledge, and perhaps most importantly, our commitment to ideals and values. With care, forethought and planning, the Southern Appalachians could be wilder, ecologically healthier and more beautiful tomorrow than they are today. It would change history to hand future generations a part of America in better ecological condition than when we inherited it. I can think of no better place to begin than the rich, blue, hazy mountains of the Southern Appalachians.

Facing page: The sparkling night-time lights of Asheville, North Carolina.

JEFF GNASS

Above: *Mabry Grist Mill, one of the attractions of the Blue Ridge Parkway in Virginia.*

Facing page: *Linville Gorge, one of the deepest in the East, is located just off the Blue Ridge Parkway in North Carolina.*

APPALACHIANS GUIDE

BLUE RIDGE PARKWAY

The Blue Ridge Parkway is a 469-mile linear park. The two-lane scenic road traverses some of the finest scenery in the Southern Appalachian Mountains. Beginning near Waynesboro, Virginia at Rockfish Gap, just south of Shenandoah National Park, the Blue Ridge Parkway winds across gaps and ridges south to Great Smoky Mountains National Park in North Carolina. For the first part of the journey, the parkway follows the crest of the Blue Ridge Mountains, then it crosses to the Black Range, Craggy and Balsam mountains before terminating on the Oconaluftee River in Great Smoky Mountains National Park. The roadway was largely constructed by hand and with primitive tools and machinery, by the Civilian Conservation Corps during the 1930s.

Following the crest of the Blue Ridge, the parkway corridor rides over ancient metamorphic and igneous rocks typical of the Blue Ridge Physiographic Province, including greenstones, schists, granites, gneisses and quartzites. You won't see any sedimentary rocks here, because the metamorphic and igneous rocks of the Blue Ridge have been thrust over younger sedimentary rocks. Usually, the youngest rocks are nearest the surface; however, in the Southern Appalachians a major thrust-fault shoved the older rocks on top of the younger strata beneath.

The resulting mountain uplands provide for spectacular elevational differences. The parkway's low point is 649 feet, along the James River, while the highest reach of the road at Richland Balsams is 6,053 feet. This elevational range ensures great variation in seasonal displays. For instance, wildflowers begin blooming in March at lower elevations and may not reach their peak at the highest elevations until June. In the fall, the situation is reversed, with leaf color on trees at the highest elevations bursting into autumn display as early as mid-September and continuing until early November at the lowest elevations.

This great elevation span also means that the parkway corridor includes a tremendous diversity of vegetative communities, ranging from southern hardwoods like catalpa and sycamore along the low-elevation river bottoms to high-elevation spruce-fir forests. There are corresponding differences in wildlife as well, with the wood thrush, for example, common in the low to mid-elevations, while its ecological equivalent on the highest peaks is the veery.

Highlights along the parkway include the James River and Kanawha Canal, where an interpretative trail explains the workings of the canal locks. Mabry Mill at milepost 176 is a restored gristmill and blacksmith shop where pioneer skills are demonstrated. Flat Rock at mile 308 offers spectacular views of Grandfather Mountain. Linville Falls at milepost 316 preserves a portion of the Linville River gorge and a magnificent falls. A bit farther, at milepost 355, is Mt. Mitchell State Park, where a side road leads to the summit of the highest mountain east of the Mississippi. At milepost 363 are the Craggy Gardens, a high ridge covered with purple rhododendron that reaches full bloom in mid-June. The parkway's highest point, Richland Balsams, is at milepost 431. Many of the white snags seen here are Fraser fir killed by insects.

In 1988 more than 25 million people drove or visited the parkway in North Carolina alone. It is particularly popular in the autumn when fall foliage provides a visual treat.

SHENANDOAH NATIONAL PARK

Shenandoah National Park straddles the narrow northern portion of the Blue Ridge Mountains—here no more than a ridge or two wide. The width of the park varies considerably, from 13.2 miles at its widest point to less than a mile at its narrowest. The 70-mile length of the park is traced by the Skyline Drive, the northern extension of the Blue Ridge Parkway. Following the ridges, this drive offers magnificent views of the piedmont to the

GEORGE WUERTHNER

85

Above: *Dark Hollow Falls, Shenandoah National Park, Virginia.*

Facing page: *On Bald River, Bald River Gorge Wilderness, Cherokee National Forest, Tennessee.*

build campgrounds and picnic areas, control erosion, install water lines and build trails.

The CCC helped put the park back on the road to ecological recovery, and today it stands as testimony to the healing powers of nature and the relatively benign climate of the region. Loggers took out most of the big timber and, except for a few isolated stands in regions too steep for logging, little old-growth forest remained. When the park was established, nearly a third of it was open grazing land with no trees are all. In this climate and region, it takes approximately 75 years for a meadow to revert to mature forest, and today 95 percent of the park is reforested.

Wildlife recovered along with forest vegetation. After the first white settlers entered the region, many of the larger mammals were extirpated, including cougar, wolf, black bear, elk and even whitetail deer. Whitetail deer were reintroduced into the park and since then have proliferated to an estimated 5,000. Black bears have made a similar recovery, with an estimated 500 to 800 animals within the park. Unfortunately, the cougar and wolf are yet to return.

This portion of the Blue Ridge is considerably lower in elevation than areas farther south. The highest point is Hawksbill Mountain, 4,050 feet in elevation. The generally low elevation accounts for the scarcity of plant and animal species with northern affinities. Paper birch, a graceful northern tree with flaky white bark that the Indians used for constructing canoes, reaches its southern limits here. Red spruce, a conifer common in New England, is only found on Limberlost, Stony Man and Hawksbill mountains, while balsam fir, the northern ecological equivalent of Fraser fir found farther south, is found only on Stony Man, Hawksbill and Crescent Rock. The New England cottontail and red squirrel are both confined to the limited spruce-fir forests on the highest summits.

Today an average of 1.8 million people annually visit the park, with the foliage season in October the single busiest month. Despite heavy visitation, much of Shenandoah will be wilder in years to come than it was in the 1930s, since approximately 40 percent of the park is formally designated wilderness.

WITHIN SHENANDOAH NATIONAL PARK

White Oak Canyon—This canyon located at milepost 42.6 has six waterfalls. The falls are created by the Catoctin greenstone formation, a form of metamorphosed lava resistant to erosion. White Oak Falls number 1 is 86 feet high and the second-highest falls in the park. The trail to this falls passes through Limberlost, a

east and the fertile and historic Shenandoah Valley to the west. For those who prefer to walk, 95 miles of the Appalachian Trail follow the crest of the ridge, mostly parallel to the Skyline Drive.

Shenandoah National Park was established in 1935, by purchase of private lands that for more than a century had been logged, farmed, mined, grazed and hunted. In 1900, the 194,600 acres that now make up the park were home to perhaps 6,000 people. But the land was overworked and most of these folks barely eked out a living. By 1936, when the park was dedicated, only 2,250 people were living within its bounds. The average family had an income of less than $200 a year. However poor, these people were self-sufficient, growing most of what they ate and living in small log cabins they built themselves. When the government began to acquire lands for the new park, many of these people willingly moved to resettlement villages located near the boundaries.

During the 1930s, and up until 1942, the Civilian Conservation Corps worked in the park. As many as 1,000 men worked to

stand of virgin hemlock. The trees here may be 400 or more years old.

Dark Hollow Falls—This falls is located in a cool hemlock-bordered forest. The 70-foot falls flows over erosion-resistant Catoctin greenstone. It is reached by a 1.5-mile round-trip trail.

Stony Man Mountain—This 4,010-foot peak is the second highest in the park and offers outstanding views from its rocky summit of greenstone. The summit rocks exhibit some columnar jointing, formed by shrinkage of the lava as it cooled. This is a good place to see high-elevation forests of spruce and fir.

Fort Windham Rocks—Tors are isolated erosion-resistant rock formations left after weathering has removed weaker rock material. These greenstone tor formations, as high as 40 feet and separated into fin-like knobs, lie upon the granitic rocks of the Pedlar Formation.

Overall Run Falls—At 93 feet, Overall Run Falls is the highest falls in the park. Located a mile and a half from Matthews Arm Campground, this falls spills over a ledge of erosion-resistant greenstone. Downstream a very rugged gorge has more cascades and cove-hardwood forests.

Old Rag Mountain—Old Rag is one of the most popular hiking destinations in the park. It offers outstanding views of the entire Blue Ridge from its summit. The mountain is largely made up of granite. Lying east of the Blue Ridge crest, Old Rag is accessible by trail from the Skyline Drive. The summit trail follows a ridgeline, with many boulders and rocks to clamber over and around—the result of weathering along joints or cracks in the bedrock. Erosion removed softer rocks, and left the harder ones as raised boulders. Dikes—rocks intruded into the existing bedrock—cross portions of the ridge.

Hawksbill Mountain—At 4,050 feet, Hawksbill Mountain is the highest peak in Shenandoah National Park. The trail to the observation tower atop it is less than two miles long, and the views from the summit cliffs certainly make it worth the effort. Northern forest species not typically found in the park, including red spruce and three-toothed cinquefoil, are found here.

Bearface Mountain—Bearface Mountain, the third-highest peak in the park, offers one of the most outstanding vistas. The summit ridge of greenstone is weathered, rugged and ragged.

Doyle River Falls—Doyle River Falls is framed by large old-growth hemlock trees. The cascading falls drops over several greenstone ledges. Of the two major falls—upper and lower—the upper drops 28 feet, while the lower falls 63 feet. This is an excellent place to see old-growth cove hardwood forest.

GEORGE WUERTHNER PHOTOS BOTH PAGES

CHEROKEE NATIONAL FOREST—TENNESSEE

The Unaka Mountains along the Tennessee-North Carolina border largely define the borders of the 623,565-acre Cherokee National Forest. This narrow sliver of public lands—no more than five to 15 miles wide—represents the westernmost portion of the Blue Ridge Physiographic Province. The Cherokee is divided between northern and southern ranger districts by Great Smoky Mountains National Park. Some parts of the forest are extremely attenuated; for instance, the Nolichucky Ranger District is more than 50 miles long, but nowhere more than three or four miles wide.

Like all other eastern national forests, the Cherokee has been largely patched together by purchasing private holdings after the passage of the 1911 Weeks Act. As a result, 48 percent of the lands within the national forest—primarily the valleys—are still under private ownership.

The Unakas are among the highest and steepest mountains in the eastern United States, and elevations in the Cherokee Forest range from 800 feet along the Conasauga River to 6,200 feet on Roan Mountain.

The lofty heights of the Cherokee wring moisture from passing air masses, and precipitation at higher elevations may exceed

75 inches per year. Most of this moisture comes in the winter months, when day-long rainfall is common. Short but intense thundershowers characterize summer precipitation.

This annual precipitation feeds nine major rivers—Little Tennessee, Nolichucky, Hiwassee, Tellico, Ocoee, South Holston, Watauga, Pigeon and French Broad. Some of these rivers are well known throughout the East for their whitewater and support a major river-rafting industry.

The rivers of the Cherokee Forest are nationally significant and eight of them—Conasauga, Ocoee, Hiwassee, Tellico, French Broad, Doe, Watauga, Nolichucky—are eligible for classification as National Wild and Scenic Rivers.

While the Cherokee rivers get the majority of recreational use in the forest, there is an abundance of hiking opportunities as well. The forest has 574 miles of trails, including 100-plus miles of the Appalachian Trail, the Overmountain Victory National Historic Trail, Warrior's Passage National Recreation Trail and John Muir National Recreation Trail.

Wilderness areas in the Cherokee include Big Laurel Branch, Pond Mountain, Sampson Mountain, Unaka Mountain, Bald River Gorge, Citico Creek and Gee Creek. Several other wilderness areas in other national forests overlap the Cherokee, including parts of the Joyce Kilmer-Slickrock, Cohutta and Big Frog wilderness areas.

For those who enjoy a pleasure drive, the very first designated National Forest Scenic Byway lies within the Cherokee National Forest. This 26-mile drive includes a 19-mile section of Highway 64 along the Ocoee River, and a 7-mile drive up Chilhowee Mountain. Highway 64 follows the Old Copper Road, which served as a main route during the 1850s to 1870s for ore wagons traveling from the copper mines at Ducktown and Copperhill to the railhead at Cleveland. From the Chilhowee Mountain road, it's possible to see the Tennessee Valley to the east, with the Cumberland Plateau beyond.

Nearly all of the national forest was logged 50 to 70 years ago and today only eight percent of the trees are estimated to be more than 80 years old. Dominant species include yellow poplar, white oak and northern red oak, along with black gum, black oak and eastern hemlock. Also found are white pine, Virginia pine, pitch pine, table mountain pine, shortleaf pine, sugar maple, yellow birch, basswood, red maple, black cherry and hickory.

Sixty-six percent of the Cherokee consists of upland or cove hardwood forests, which produce an abundance of mast crops— important food for deer, wild turkey, black bear and other wild-

life. The high mast crop, along with sufficient secure unroaded terrain, supports the only significant black bear population in Tennessee outside of Great Smoky Mountains National Park.

Timber harvest is a primary focus of most national forests. However, the real value of the Cherokee is not timber production, but its role in preserving biodiversity. Some 384 vertebrate species occur in the Cherokee National Forest, including 47 mammals such as opossum, raccoon, gray squirrel, red squirrel, mink and bobcat. Thirty reptile species and 46 amphibian species flourish here.

The Cherokee is also home to 135 species of fish—one of the greatest diversities of finned creatures in any national forest in the nation. Nearly 347 miles of wild trout waters are found here, including some of the best native brook trout waters in Tennessee. Special effort is focused on the brook trout, and its restoration in all suitable waters is one of the major fishery management goals of the forest.

National forest waterways are also home to several endangered or threatened fish species. These include the Smoky madtom, thought extinct until discovered in a small stretch of stream in 1980. Other rare fish species include the Conasauga logperch found in the Conasauga River, and yellowfin madtom found in Citico Creek.

The Cherokee National Forest's proximity to Great Smoky Mountains National Park and the adjacent Nantahala and Pisgah national forests in North Carolina makes management of these forest and park lands critical to the long-term health of the Southern Appalachian bioregion.

WITHIN THE CHEROKEE NATIONAL FOREST

Watauga Scenic Area—The 1,100-acre Watauga Scenic Area is located east of Elizabethtown near Watauga Lake. The area is now part of the Pond Mountain Wilderness and contains some fine examples of old-growth hemlock and hardwood trees— many 38 to 40 inches in diameter. The highest point is 4,329-foot Pond Mountain, which has rugged rock outcrops with excellent views.

Unaka Mountain Scenic Area—The 360-acre Unaka Mountain area, now part of the Unaka Mountain Wilderness east of Erwin, was severely burned in 1925. In many areas bare rock is still exposed. Rhododendron and flame azalea are abundant and are especially lovely during the spring flowering season. On the southeast portion of the mountain a virgin stand of huge old-growth red spruce has some trees up to 40 inches in diameter.

Facing page: Witch hazel, Citico Wilderness, Cherokee National Forest.

Rock Creek Gorge—Eleven waterfalls in a rugged gorge are the prime attractions of this 220-acre area near Lake Ocoee. One of these falls cascades more than 180 feet.

Coker Creek Scenic Area—This 375-acre area contains a four-and-a-half-mile gorge along Coker Creek. Accessible only by foot, the stream is characterized by pools and waterfalls interspersed with huge boulders. Due to the rugged terrain, the area has stands of old-growth eastern hemlock and white pine, plus an abundance of flowering shrubs such as flame azalea, rhododendron and mountain laurel.

Bald Mountain Ridge—Located along the state line, this mountainous area has 60-percent–grade slopes, with the highest point found at 4,830-foot Big Butt. Several open balds characterize the higher portions of the mountain. At lower elevations, Jennings Creek pours over a series of picturesque rock shelves.

Moffett Laurel—This wetlands of the Unaka Ranger District is located at 4,000 feet elevation near the Appalachian Trail. The wet terrain precluded logging and the area is dominated by mature hemlock trees. It is host to a number of unusual plant communities, and is listed by the Forest Service as a potential botanical area.

Gentry Creek—This 1,297-acre area has elevations reaching almost 5,000 feet. Numerous open balds characterize it, while Gentry Creek has a scenic double waterfall and good trout fishing.

Big Frog Wilderness—This 7,972-acre wilderness lies just north of the Georgia border. Although small, the area is contiguous to the much larger, 35,247-acre Cohutta Wilderness in Georgia. Big Frog Mountain (4,224 feet in elevation) is the most prominent feature. Rolling hills dominate this area south of the Ocoee River. Drained by Rough Creek, Indian Creek and other tributaries of the Ocoee, the wilderness area is accessible by eight hiking trails totaling 26 miles.

Gee Creek Wilderness—Three hiking trails traverse the 2,493-acre Gee Creek Wilderness. Despite a relatively modest elevational difference of 1,500 feet between the highest and lowest points, the Gee Creek area is nevertheless characterized by its steep terrain. Fishing in Gee Creek is good for brown trout.

Big Laurel Branch Wilderness—The 6,251-acre Big Laurel Wilderness lies in the northern portion of the Cherokee National Forest southeast of Tennessee Highway 91 by Elizabethtown. Drained by its namesake, Big Laurel Creek, this area is characterized by steep topography, with narrow ridges separated by hollows, and it holds an abundance of waterfalls and cascades. Cliffs

Above: Hiker on Pickens Nose, Southern Nantahala Wilderness, North Carolina.

Facing page: Rappeling down Seneca Rocks as part of National Youth Science Camp.

and open ridgetops provide numerous opportunities for scenic views. The Appalachian Trail traverses the area. One of the more unusual species found here is scattered stands of Carolina hemlock.

Sampson Mountain Wilderness—This 8,319-acre wilderness lies right along the Tennessee-North Carolina border east of Greenville. With elevations ranging from 2,000 feet to 4,838 feet at Big Butt Mountain, this area has many steep, rugged slopes. On the upper reaches of Clark Creek is Buckeye Falls, reputed to be the highest waterfall in the eastern U.S. This is one of the major black bear areas in Tennessee.

Pond Mountain Wilderness—This 6,665-acre wilderness area varies in elevation from 1,900 to 4,329 feet on Pond Mountain. Attractions include the Laurel Fork Gorge with its scenic waterfalls and the 40-foot cascade of Laurel Fork Falls. Some limited stands of virgin timber remain on some upper ridges. The Watauga Scenic Area is now part of this wilderness. The Appalachian Trail and several other trails go through the area.

Unaka Mountain Wilderness—This 4,700-acre area is northeast of Erwin on the Tennessee-North Carolina border. Highest elevation is at The Overlook, a 4,860-foot prominence. Attractions include the vistas from the ridgetops, the more than 10 waterfalls greater than 20 feet in height including 60-foot Red Fork Falls, and virgin stands of eastern hemlock.

Bald River Gorge Wilderness—This 3,887-acre wilderness east of Tellico Plains protects the scenic Bald River Gorge. Many people view the 120-foot Bald River Falls only from the northern boundary of the wilderness; however, the hike along the river within the wilderness is relatively easy. The trail passes many deep pools interspersed by beautiful cascades and small falls.

Citico Creek Wilderness—The 16,000-acre Citico Creek Wilderness lying on the Tennessee-North Carolina border east of Tellico Plains is the largest wilderness in the Cherokee National Forest. However, Citico Creek is contiguous to the 17,000-acre Joyce Kilmer-Slickrock Wilderness, so the effective size of this area is quite large. Elevations range from 1,400 to 5,120 feet, so relief is quite substantial, resulting in an abundance of waterfalls and cascades that includes the 80-foot Falls Branch Falls. Most of the area was logged during the 1920s and 1930s. A few virgin stands of timber remain in the more remote areas, including a beech-maple forest in the Falls Branch area and a hemlock-hardwood stand near Glenn Gap. The Citico is important as a roadless refuge for black bear.

Little Frog Mountain Wilderness—Low foothills and a long north-south ridge characterize the 4,800-acre Little Frog Mountain Wilderness located east of Parksville. Little Frog Mountain is a long ridge whose highest summit is 3,322 feet in elevation. The major creeks—Laurel Branch, Rock Creek, Williams Creek and Johnson Creek—all drain into the Ocoee River. There are two trails in the area.

NANTAHALA AND PISGAH NATIONAL FORESTS—NORTH CAROLINA

The 1,015,330 mountainous acres of the Nantahala and Pisgah national forests encompass a large proportion of the middle and upper slopes between 3,000 and 6,000 feet of the entire 18-county area of western North Carolina.

As part of the Blue Ridge physiographic province, most of the rocks are metamorphic gneisses, schists and granites. Recently, parts of the national forest were identified as part of the eastern Overthrust Belt, where oil and gas might be trapped. But, to date, no exploration has occurred.

These forests represent a major natural depository for biological diversity, with 1,885 plants known to occur on these lands. At higher elevations are some of the most extensive spruce-fir forests in the Southern Appalachians. On many of the peaks above 5,000 feet are "balds"—unusual plant communities dominated by grasses and shrubby heaths. However, far and away the most common plant community is the hardwood forest, which makes up 80 percent of the timber cover. Like most eastern national forests, these lands were purchased from timber companies after the turn of the century, consequently most of the trees are rather young. Only 12 percent of the forest is more than 80 years old, while the majority (72 percent) is between 40 and 80 years old.

This diversity of plant communities supports 645 species of vertebrates, including fish. Since these forests, along with Great Smoky Mountains National Park, are the region's only large land parcels sufficiently free from human disturbance, they are extremely important as habitat for wide-ranging species like the black bear. Other wildlife found on national forest lands include: northern flying squirrel, whitetail deer, pileated woodpecker, gray fox, bobcat, wild turkey, raven, spotfin chub and brook trout.

Some areas of the national forest receive more than 80 inches of precipitation a year, and high-quality water may be the most valuable resource produced by these forests. Thirteen municipal watersheds rise on these forest lands.

The high-quality water also fuels the local recreation economy. Some rivers, such as the Nantahala and Nolichucky, are well known by whitewater enthusiasts. But river running is not the only recreational use of forest waterways. Two thousand miles of trout fisheries include some native brook trout waters.

By far, the most important aspect of the forest is its value for preservation of ecological systems. This preservation has economic value as well, since pure water, clean air and preservation of genetic diversity have long-term economic implications. However, in the more limited definition of local economic values, recreation still outpaces logging. The Forest Service timber program provides only one percent of the timber cut in North Carolina annually; wages in mills contribute but 0.2 percent of the economy.

The abundance of waterfalls, gorges, blads, cliffs, peaks and highly scenic terrain is a major tourist draw. Both the Blue Ridge Parkway and Appalachian Trail wind through portions of these forests and not surprisingly, tourism is a major and growing regional industry.

There are six designated wilderness areas: Linville Gorge, Joyce Kilmer-Slickrock, Ellicott Rock, Southern Nantahala, Middle Prong and Shining Rock. In addition, five other roadless areas are under consideration for wilderness designation including: Upper Wilson Creek, Craggy Mountain, Harper Creek, Lost Cove, Overflow, Cheoah Bald and Snowbird.

WITHIN THE NANTAHALA NATIONAL FOREST

Buck Creek Serpentine Barrens—A belt of serpentine rocks crosses parts of North Carolina and Georgia. Only a limited number of plant species can tolerate the chemical composition of these outcrops and, as a consequence, the forest of stunted pitch pine and grass is noticeably different from the surrounding hardwoods. Several grasses found here are more typical of the Midwest than of the South.

Chattooga River Gorge— The Chattooga is a designated Wild and Scenic River flowing through Ellicott Rock Wilderness Area. The river eventually leaves North Carolina to form the border between Georgia and South Carolina. A scenic gorge complete with cascades and rapids flows through a break in the Blue Ridge escarpment.

Joyce Kilmer Forest— Since most of the Southern Appalachians were logged shortly after the turn of the century, few examples of old-growth forest are left, but one of the finest stands has been protected within the Joyce Kilmer Memorial Forest, named for the man who composed the poem "Trees." Hemlocks up to 70 inches in diameter, along with huge yellow poplar 76 inches or more in diameter and up to a hundred feet tall, grow along Santeetlah Creek in the Unicoi Mountains.

Whitewater Falls and Gorge—One of the most spectacular waterfalls in the Southern Appalachians is the aptly named Whitewater Falls on the North Carolina-South Carolina border. The Whitewater River cuts through the Blue Ridge Escarpment and plummets more than 800 feet in Upper and Lower Falls.

Whiteside Mountain—Some of the largest cliff faces in the entire Southern Appalachians are found on the north, south and east sides of Whiteside Mountain. The mountain rises 2,100 feet above its base to the 4,930-foot summit that offers spectacular views. A dwarf northern red oak forest dominates the dry summit area.

Cullasaja River Gorge—The Cullasaja River has one of the finest collections of waterfalls in North Carolina, including the 150-foot Cullasaja Falls, and the 80-foot Dry Falls. In total, six major falls occur within the seven-mile gorge.

Cheoah Bald Proposed Wilderness—Cheoah Bald stands 5,100 feet high, rising dramatically over the Nantahala River Gorge near Robbinsville. The Appalachian Trail crosses this 21,400-acre roadless area.

Southern Nantahala Wilderness—Rising to 5,499 feet on Standing Indian Mountain, the rugged mountains of the 24,515-acre Southern Nantahala Wilderness straddle two states—North Carolina and Georgia—and encompass the headwaters of a number of rivers including the Nantahala, Hiwassee and Tallulah. Five shelters and 32 miles of the Appalachian Trail form a ridgeline corridor, while 14 other trails provide access to other parts of the wilderness. More than 17,000 acres of roadless lands could be added to the existing wilderness to create a 42,000-acre wilderness—potentially one of the largest in the Southern Appalachians. Timber sales on Indian Ridge and Chunky Gal Mountain threaten this proposed expansion.

Joyce Kilmer-Slickrock Wilderness—The 17,013-acre Joyce Kilmer-Slickrock Wilderness lies in the Unicoi Mountains on the Tennessee border with its lowest point at 1,086 feet, while the highest, Stratton Bald, tops out at 5,300 feet. Much of what is now wilderness was bought in 1915 by Babcock Lumber Company and logged. A logging railroad once ran up Slickrock Creek. In contrast, much of the Little Santeetlah Creek watershed was never logged and the large old-growth forests in the Joyce Kilmer Memorial Forest present a rare opportunity to view this forest community.

WITHIN THE PISGAH NATIONAL FOREST

Roan Mountain—Located on the Tennessee-North Carolina border, Roan Mountain is a massive 10-mile-long upland ridge whose 6,286-foot summit is a grassy bald. At one time a 166-room hotel, the "Cloudland," attracted guests from the surrounding lowlands. Roan Mountain has forests of red spruce-

GLENN VAN NIMWEGEN

Fraser fir as well as extensive balds. There are a number of outstanding and beautiful floral displays on the mountain including the largest purple rhododendron garden in North America. The Appalachian Trail follows the summit ridgeline, and many consider this section to be the most spectacular on the entire trail.

Big Bald Mountain—The 5,516-foot open summit of Big Bald Mountain provides one of the most outstanding panoramas in the entire Southern Appalachians. This grassy bald is home to several rare plants including Roan Mountain bluet, Roan Mountain rattlesnake root and moss pink phlox. In addition, the southern slope has a fine example of old-growth northern red oak forest. The Appalachian Trail provides access to this area.

Looking Glass Rock—Like the better-known Stone Mountain, the rounded granite dome of Looking Glass Rock is a fine example of exfoliation or the peeling away of rock layers. Rising 1,500 feet above the surrounding forest, the distinctive bare rock cliffs are visible from the Blue Ridge Parkway.

Craggy Gardens—The rugged rocky ridges of the Craggys are well known for more than a dozen rare plants, plus ridgetop rhododendron floral displays in June. There are also fine small patches of old-growth hemlock and northern hardwood forests. The area is reached via the Blue Ridge Parkway.

Linville Gorge Wilderness—The 10,975-acre Linville Gorge Wilderness is one of the deepest gorges found in the Southeast—some claim it is the deepest gorge east of the Mississippi. The rugged terrain discouraged logging and, as a consequence, this area has some of the best examples of virgin old-growth eastern hemlock found in the national forest. Waterfalls, deep pools and riffles characterize the Linville River, a good trout stream.

Shining Rock Wilderness—At the head of the West Prong of the Pigeon River, southwest of Asheville and north and west of the Blue Ridge Parkway, lie the 18,500 acres of the Shining Rock Wilderness, named for outcrops of white quartz. The wilderness is mountainous, with high, bald ridges and five peaks above 6,000 feet. Logging, in combination with severe fires in 1925 and 1942, stripped the peaks of trees and created grassy balds that persist today. Many of the trails in the area are revegetated railroad grades from the logging era.

Upper Wilson Creek Proposed Wilderness—Located just north of the popular Linville Gorge Wilderness, the 6,500-acre proposed Upper Wilson Creek Wilderness has a native trout fishery and is important black bear habitat. The creek itself was studied as a potential addition to the Wild and Scenic River system and for designation as an Outstanding Resource Water in the state of North Carolina. At this writing, no action has been taken on it.

Middle Prong Wilderness—The 7,900-acre Middle Prong Wilderness is bordered on the south by the Blue Ridge Parkway. This area, at the headwaters of the Middle Prong of the Pigeon River, is mountainous with several major ridges. There are three trails within the wilderness—two accessing grassy balds, while another follows the Middle Prong of the Pigeon River.

CHATTAHOOCHEE NATIONAL FOREST—GEORGIA

The 741,400-acre Chattahoochee National Forest lies in northern Georgia and encompasses the southern end of the Appalachian Range. However, this represents only 45 percent of the land within the authorized purchase area boundaries. This is one of the first uplands that air masses encounter in moving inland from the nearby Atlantic Ocean. Precipitation is heavy—more than 80 inches annually at some of the higher elevations. Most of the forest is within the Blue Ridge Mountains physiographic region with its metamorphic granites, gneisses and schists. However, the portion west of Dalton is part of the Ridge and Valley province dominated by sedimentary rocks.

White pine is more common here than in forests farther north due to the overall warmer climatic conditions, but this spe-

Above: Looking Glass Rock, Pisgah National Forest, North Carolina.

Facing page: Craggy Gardens, Blue Ridge Parkway, North Carolina.

Reflections in an old beaver pond along the Conasauga River, Cohutta Wilderness, Chattahoochee National Forest, Georgia.

came farmers, who overgrazed and overworked the land. Soil erosion and the resulting decline in productivity gradually ended farming. Lumber companies came next to the region, and within 30 years had stripped the mountains of nearly all the accessible timber. By 1936, when the Chattahoochee National Forest was established, most of the land now held by the federal government had been cut over. As a result, little old-growth timber remains except for small pockets overlooked by the loggers.

Fortunately, the warm, moist climate is conducive to forest growth. Most of the Chattahoochee is now reforested and gradually acquiring a higher percentage of mature-forest types. But timber production is no longer the dominant use of the forest. Given its location less than two hours from Atlanta, one of the most important resources of the Chattahoochee National Forest is recreation. The Appalachian Trail's southern terminus is on Springer Mountain, and 79 miles of the trail are located within the Chattahoochee. Several other nationally known trails include the 37-mile Bartram Trail that follows the path pioneer naturalist William Bartram took across Georgia in the 1700s. The 53-mile Benton MacKaye Trail, named for the originator of the Appalachian Trail concept, goes from the Tennessee state line to Springer Mountain.

Nine wilderness areas, totaling 88,519 acres, compose 17 percent of the total forest acreage. The designated wilderness areas include Big Frog, Brasstown, Cohutta, Ellicott Rock, Raven Cliffs, Rich Mountain, Southern Nantahala, and Tray Mountain. The Chattooga Wild and Scenic River flows through a portion of the Chattahoochee National Forest, and 15 other rivers have been identified as potential additions to the Wild and Scenic River system.

WITHIN THE CHATTAHOOCHEE NATIONAL FOREST

Brasstown Bald—Georgia's highest mountain is 4,784-foot Brasstown Bald. A visitor center and tower on the summit provide views on clear days of four states. Two national recreation trails—Jacks Knob Trail and Arkaquah Trail—converge on the summit, and a steep road provides auto and bus access. Although the peak is in the southern state of Georgia, a record low temperature of minus 27 degrees Fahrenheit once was recorded here.

Anna Ruby Falls—Below Tray Mountain lie the twin falls of Anna Ruby Falls, headwaters of the Appalachicola River. Curtis Creek drops 153 feet, while York Creek tumbles 50 feet. Named by Civil War Colonel John Nichols for his daughter, the falls and surrounding land were purchased by the federal govern-

cies still constitutes only 8 percent of the forest community. Other important tree species include white and red oak, hickory and yellow poplar. Approximately 48 percent of the forest is upland-mixed hardwoods, while only 16 percent is cove hardwood.

Biological diversity is one of the Chattahoochee National Forest's attributes. There are, for instance, more than 500 wildlife species here. Some of the mammals and birds of note are otter, bobcat, mink, beaver, ruffed grouse, bog turtle, pileated woodpecker, dusky salamander, yellow fin shiner, brook trout, Coosa darter, whitetail deer and wild turkey. The Chattahoochee is particularly important as black bear habitat, since large-bole trees are critical for denning. Maintaining old-growth timber stands is thus critical to the bear's survival.

The area now part of the Chattahoochee National Forest was inhabited by the Cherokee Indians between 1500 and 1800. Then, in the 1820s and 1830s—with a major rush in 1828—gold was discovered in these north Georgia mountains and prospectors moved into the region. Following on the heels of the miners

ment in 1925 and now are part of a 1,600-acre scenic area. A 0.4-mile trails leads from a parking lot to the falls.

DeSoto Falls—Five waterfalls tumble along a three-mile stretch of DeSoto Creek within a 650-acre recreation area. The creek is named for the Spanish explorer, Hernando DeSoto, who passed through this region in the 1500s.

Cohutta Wilderness—Within the core of the Cohutta Mountains, the 35,247-acre Cohutta Wilderness lies on the Georgia-Tennessee border. Immediately north of the Georgia border is the Big Frog Wilderness in Tennessee, effectively enlarging this roadless area by more than 8,000 additional acres.

The Cohutta Mountains are relatively rugged with a fair amount of relief. The lowest point is 950 feet along the Alaculsey Valley, while Big Frog Mountain, at 4,200 feet, is the highest summit. Laced with 90 miles of trails, this area is large enough to provide relatively long wilderness trips. With as much as 80 inches of precipitation annually, water is abundant—and both the Conasauga and Jack's River offer trout fishing.

Seventy percent of the area was logged between 1915 and 1930. Railroads were built with hand tools and hard labor, up the Conasauga and Jack's Rivers and along their tributaries. Many of these old railroad beds are now trails. The Forest Service began to acquire the lands here in 1934.

Tray Mountain Wilderness—Tray Mountain, at 4,430 feet, is the high point of the 9,702-acre Tray Mountain Wilderness which lies north of Helen, Georgia. Rocky gorges and cascading streams are found throughout the area. Annual precipitation is heavy, and averages more than 78 inches on top of Tray Mountain. The Appalachian Trail passes through the area. Several rare or threatened species of plants occur here, and native brook trout inhabit some of the streams.

Brasstown Bald Wilderness—Brasstown Bald, the highest peak in Georgia, is just outside this 11,405-acre wilderness. Several National Recreation Trails, including the Arkaqua and the Jacks Knobs, along with the Appalachian Trail, pass through the area. Wildlife and plants unusual and rare for Georgia occur here, including the raven, pygmy shrew and New England cottontail. Five rare species of plants, several of them orchids, grow here.

Rich Mountain Wilderness—The 9,649-acre Rich Mountain Wilderness lies between the towns of Blue Ridge and Ellijay, Georgia. Elevations vary from 1,700 feet to 4,000 feet. High peaks form the center of the wilderness with drainages radiating out from them. Having no trails, this area is a valuable biological preserve since human influence is low.

Mountain ash frames the view from Brasstown Bald, highest point in Georgia. Chattahoochee National Forest.

Raven Cliffs Wilderness—The 8,532-acre Raven Cliffs Wilderness straddles the crest of the Blue Ridge and includes the Raven Cliffs Scenic Area. Elevations vary from 1,800 feet, to 3,846 feet on Leveland Mountain. Waterfalls, cliffs and rugged mountains typify this area. The Appalachian Trail follows the crest for 6.6 miles through here. Forty-one miles of trout streams include native brook trout populations.

MONOGAHELA NATIONAL FOREST—WEST VIRGINIA

The 875,000-acre Monongahela National Forest is located in eastern West Virginia along the Virginia border. The area is extremely mountainous, part of the Ridge and Valley as well as Allegheny Plateau physiographic provinces, with elevations ranging from 900 feet near Petersburg to 4,860 atop Spruce Knob, the highest point in West Virginia.

The highlands of the Monongahela Forest present a barrier

95

GEORGE WUERTHNER

96

to the passage of moisture-laden air moving eastward from the Ohio River Valley and, as a consequence, a great deal of precipitation is wrung from clouds as they move over the mountains. The west slope of the forest may get as much as 60 inches of precipitation a year, while valleys in the lee of the mountain front along the Virginia border often get half that much.

As with all the national forests in the eastern United States, these lands had to be purchased from private owners. The first lands in the Monongahela were bought in 1915, and federal acquisition continues today. Almost half the land within the purchase bounds of the Monongahela Forest still is privately owned. In a state where human development dominates, most West Virginians view the Monongahela National Forest as a special and unique place providing rare recreation and scenic opportunities.

Some of the forest has been given special recognition for its scenic or wilderness characteristics. For instance, five designated wilderness areas—including Dolly Sods, Otter Brook, South Laurel, North Laurel and Cranberry—total 78,000 acres or approximately nine percent of the forest. There are also seven National Natural Landmarks, two scenic areas and the Spruce Knob-Seneca Rocks National Recreation Area.

For those who wish to drive, not walk, more than 3,400 miles of road comb the forest—although, at any one time, not all may be open for public travel. According to the preferred alternative in the Monongahela Forest Plan, another 400 miles of roads will be built or reconstructed during the next decade.

The large blocks of public lands provide critical habitat for many species, including endangered or threatened ones like the northern flying squirrel, Indian bat and Virginia big-eared bat. Other species, like the Cheat Mountain salamander, have extremely limited distribution: this species is known from only 50 sites on the forest. Although the forest accounts for less than 10 percent of the area of West Virginia, it provides 40 percent of the state's wild turkey habitat and 80 percent of black bear habitat. Altogether, 1,500 species of plants and 374 species of animals are found on the forest.

Five major forest communities are represented on the Monongahela, with 75 tree species. Oak-hickory and maple-beech-birch associations account for 80 percent of the forest.

At the highest elevations are found nearly pure stands of red spruce. Most of West Virginia's red spruce is found within the forest's higher elevations. But, prior to heavy logging and fires that occurred at the turn of the century, red spruce occupied nearly 470,000 acres of the forest. The remaining spruce provides important habitat for a number of species otherwise not found in the region, including snowshoe hare, a number of salamanders, and wood warbler.

Northern hardwood forests crowd the spruce at the highest elevations. These are the same hardwood trees species one might typically see in Vermont or Maine, and include sugar maple, beech, red maple, yellow birch, and understory species like striped maple, hobblebush and viburnums.

At lower elevations and drier elevations are found the oaks and hickories. On the Monongahela, important oaks include northern red, black, scarlet, chestnut and white. Each species produces acorns, an important food for wildlife.

On the deep, rich, moist soils along streams and lower elevation slopes are the cove hardwoods more typical of the southern Appalachians, including yellow poplar, cucumber tree, elm, basswood and black locust. Due to the rich soils, in the past many of these sites had been cleared and supported small farms.

On sites that have been logged several times in the past, one finds the Allegheny hardwood forests. Besides sugar maple, yellow birch and red maple, this type also has black cherry, white ash and other species.

WITHIN THE MONONGAHELA NATIONAL FOREST

Spruce Knob-Seneca Rocks National Recreation Area (NRA) encompasses 100,000 acres at the headwaters of the Potomac River. Within the NRA is Spruce Knob, highest point in West Virginia. Here an observation tower enables visitors to get above the tallest trees, and the views from the rocky, open summit are spectacular. As its name implies, red spruce dominates this alpine area, along with huckleberry, blueberry and mountain ash. Fifty-eight miles of hiking trails lace this unit of the NRA together.

Seneca Rocks rises more than 1,000 feet above the headwaters of the North Fork of the South Branch of the Potomac River. The rugged cliffs of Seneca Rocks are considered one of the best vertical climbs in the eastern United States.

Cranberry Wilderness—Encompassing the drainages of the Williams and Cranberry rivers, which dissect uplands of the Allegheny Plateau, is the 35,864-acres Cranberry Wilderness. Named for high-elevation cranberry bogs, the wilderness is also habitat for species more typical of northern environments, like dwarf dogwood, buckbean, bog rosemary and goldthread. Wildlife includes hermit thrush, northern water thrush, bobcat, black bear, turkey and snowshoe hare.

Above: Dolly Sods Wilderness, Monongahela National Forest, West Virginia.
Left: Flowers frame Seneca Rocks. Monongahela National Forest.

Facing page: Sunset from Spruce Knob, highest point in West Virginia, Monongahela National Forest.

Another 45,000 acres of roadless lands, including the Cranberry back country, surround the designated wilderness, bringing the total roadless lands to more than 80,000 acres, easily the largest wildlands area of the forest.

Cranberry Glades Botanical Area—The Cranberry Glades are open sphagnum moss bogs, representing areas with poor drainage and acidic conditions that limit decomposition. The 600 acres are home to plants more typical of northern New England bogs, including insect-eating plants like pitcher plant and sundew. A board walk allows visitors to explore the glades without stepping on fragile vegetation.

The most prominent plant is the scarlet sphagnum moss. Sphagnum slowly grows upward, covering moss and other plants that have died. Eventually, if enough time passes, these dead, undecomposed plants will form peat. The moss is extremely absorbent and, in the past, Indians used it for diapers. If you squeeze a handful of sphagnum, icy, tannin-stained, water gushes as if from a sponge.

Otter Brook Wilderness—Forty miles of trails lace the 20,000-acre Otter Brook Wilderness, and some of them require wading Otter Brook. Most of the area is covered with second-growth forests resulting from timber harvests near the turn of the 20th century as well as between 1958 and 1972.

Dolly Sods Wilderness—Red spruce and eastern hemlock up to three and four feet in diameter once covered the 10,215-acre Dolly Sods Wilderness. The area was logged near the turn of the century, and later was swept by fires that eliminated much of the organic humus. Today, a smaller, shrubby, second-growth forest is slowly revegetating much of the area.

Sods is another term for pastures, which local farmers maintained by burning and grazing. The area was grazed by cattle belonging to a pioneer family named Dahle. The Dahle was corrupted into Dolly—hence the name, Dolly Sods.

One gets a sensation of being in a northern environment here. Like the Cranberry Glades to the south, the Dolly Sods area contains sphagnum moss bogs with sundew and cranberries. Where they are forested, red spruce along with yellow birch and aspen dominate. But there are also extensive "plains" or open heath areas where azalea, rhododendron, blueberry and mountain laurel create openings in what would otherwise be dense forest.

Laurel Fork Wildernesses—The Laurel Fork of the Cheat River lies west of Rich Mountain and east of Middle Mountain. Forest Road 40 separates the area into a Laurel Fork South and Laurel Fork North; the combined area of both is 12,200 acres.

The area originally was owned by the Laurel River Lumber Company, which logged the virgin timber off by 1921. A railroad once ran along the river and carried the logs to mills for processing. After logging ended, several fires swept over the area, and the vegetation we see today is a direct result of the past logging and fire influences. Today the old railroad grade has been turned into a trail that follows the Laurel Fork, while several short side trails provide additional access.

Gaudineer Scenic Area—Virgin timber is exceedingly rare in the Monongahela National Forest, so the uncut spruce forest of the Gaudineer Scenic Area is particularly special. This 130-acre site provides a glimpse of what the region looked like prior to logging. Some of these spruce are more than 250 years in age, and 35 inches in diameter.

Falls of Hills Creek—Waterfalls are not in short supply over the length of the Southern Appalachians, but the three waterfalls at Hills Creek are especially lovely. Cascading in steps down a narrow gorge, Hills Creek, the highest at 65 feet, ties with Blackwater Falls as the highest falls in West Virginia.

Highlands Scenic Parkway—If driving is your pleasure, the Highlands Scenic Parkway—which begins on U.S. 219 by Marlinton and ends at the Cranberry Mountain Visitor Center on highway 55—is a mini–Blue Ridge Parkway. The Highlands Scenic Parkway is the highest major highway in West Virginia, with more than 60 percent of the road above elevations of 4,000 feet. With pullouts and vistas, the spectacular views, particularly during the autumn foliage season, are worth the detour necessary to travel this road. Commercial trucking is prohibited, and only recreational vehicles are permitted.

GEORGE WASHINGTON NATIONAL FOREST—VIRGINIA, WEST VIRGINIA

The 1,055,000-acre George Washington National Forest holds the headwaters for the Shenandoah, James and Jackson rivers. Most of the forest is in Virginia (954,000 acres), while a smaller portion (101,000 acres) lies in West Virginia. The majority of the forest is in the Valley and Ridge province west of the Great Valley (Shenandoah Valley), but the easternmost portions

Above: Laurel Brook in South Laurel Fork Wilderness, Monongahela National Forest.
Left: Cranberry Glades Botanical Area—one of the largest bogs in the Southern Appalachians. Monongahela National Forest.

Facing page: Seneca Rocks National Recreation Area, Monongahela National Forest.

Crabtree Falls on the George Washington National Wilderness, with five cascades dropping 1,200 feet, is the longest falls in Virginia.

FREDERICK D. ATWOOD

of the forest include parts of the Blue Ridge, and Massanutten Mountain. The highest elevations of the forest are just over 4,000 feet.

Precipitation varies with elevation, with some parts of the forest receiving as little as 18 inches annually, while others may receive as much as 48 inches. Overall, the forest is drier than the Monongahela Forest, which lies farther west in West Virginia. The drier conditions are reflected by its vegetation, primarily oak and hickory, with white pine dominating on some sites. Pitch pine and Table Mountain pine occupy the driest and rockiest outcrops.

The forest also has some small but unusual plant communities, including shale barrens and bogs.

It supports an abundance of wildlife, including 67 species of fish, 66 of reptiles and amphibians, 140 bird species and 57 species of mammals. Hunting and fishing account for 29 percent of forest use. It's easy to understand this demand when one considers that the George Washington holds 44 percent of Virginia's public land that is open to hunting, even though the forest composes only four percent of the state's land base.

Since the forest is within a day's drive of 54 million people, it is not surprising that recreation is its number one attraction. The Forest has 105 developed sites, including campgrounds, plus 830 miles of hiking trails (including 56 miles of the Appalachian Na-

tional Scenic Trail). Trout Pond, on the Lee Ranger District, is the only natural lake in the state of West Virginia. Lake Moomaw, Todd Lake and Sherando Lake are other water bodies on the forest. Crabtree Falls, just off the Blue Ridge Parkway, is reputed to be the highest waterfall in Virginia.

WITHIN GEORGE WASHINGTON NATIONAL FOREST

There are four wilderness areas in the George Washington Forest: St. Mary's, Ramsey's Draft, Rough Mountain and Rich Hole.

St. Mary's Wilderness Area is 10,090 acres in size. Located in the Blue Ridge just west of the Blue Ridge Parkway north of Lexington. The St. Mary's River, really only a creek, is part of Virginia's Scenic Rivers System and a designated brook trout stream. The main trail follows St. Mary's River past pools of up to 10 feet in depth and travels beside a double waterfall.

Ramsey's Draft Wilderness Area is a small (6,725 acres) wilderness that encompasses the Ramsey's Draft drainage on the slopes of Shenandoah Mountain west of Staunton. A trail follows the main river, with a branch going up Jerry's Run, while several other trails follow ridges. Ramsay's Draft and its tributaries are all designated brook trout waters.

Rough Mountain Wilderness Area is a 9,300-acre roadless area along the Cowpasture River in Bath County. The highest point is 2,842-foot Rough Mountain, while the low point lies at 1,170 feet along the Cowpasture River. The ridgetops offer good views of surrounding lowlands. The Crane Trail takes hikers over the top of the mountain.

The 6,450-acre *Rich Hole Roadless Area* lies just west of Interstate 64 near the Rockbridge-Alleghany County line. The area has some interesting rocky outcrops in the southern end, plus virgin stands of old-growth timber not logged during the last century. During the 1800s, several iron furnaces operated in the area and many trees were cut to make charcoal. Evidence of the cutting and mining operations still can be seen.

Crabtree Falls is reputed to be the longest falls in Virginia and perhaps the entire eastern United States, with a total drop of more than 1,200 feet in a series of five major cascades. The falls are located in the Blue Ridge Mountains off State Route 56. By following the trail along the falls, one eventually reaches Crabtree Meadows, where several pioneer families once lived. Here in the open area grow crabapples and apples they planted. A half mile beyond the meadows is the Appalachian Trail.

North Mountain Trail winds for 14.5 miles along the crest of Great North Mountain and offers spectacular views in all directions. The North Mountain Trail passes by Elliott Knob at 4,463 feet, one of the highest points on the entire forest. An abandoned fire lookout tower and radio and TV repeater station crown the knob.

Skidmore Natural Area—On 1,300 acres on the upper reaches of the Skidmore Fork is one the few remaining examples of virgin eastern hemlock forest left in Virginia. The area also has some fine examples of red spruce forest, unusual for the number and diversity of birds associated with it.

Mt. Pleasant Loop Trail circles both 4,021-foot Mt. Pleasant and 4,032-foot Pompey Mountain in the Blue Ridge Mountains on the Pedlar Ranger District. Besides passing many scenic vistas, the trail also traverses virgin hardwood forest in Little Cove Creek.

JEFFERSON NATIONAL FOREST—VIRGINIA, KENTUCKY, AND WEST VIRGINIA

The Jefferson National Forest stretches more than 200 miles from south of Lexington, Virginia to the North Carolina border. Spanning the Blue Ridge, Valley and Ridge and Appalachian Plateau, the forest overlaps seven major river systems: the New, Cumberland, Clinch, Holston, Big Sandy, Roanoke and James.

Most of the forest is in Virginia, with 690,254 acres covering 19 counties in that state. An additional 18,211 acres are in West Virginia, with another 961 acres just crossing into Kentucky. The lowest elevation, 600 feet, is along the James River, while Mt. Rogers at 5,729 feet is the highest point on the forest and also in the state of Virginia.

Average precipitation is only 37 inches, hence the vegetation reflects this relative aridity by the dominance of oaks and hickory. However, northern hardwood forest species like sugar maple, red maple and yellow birch are found at higher, wetter elevations. Red spruce is restricted to the highest peaks such as the summit of Whitetop Mountain.

Recreation is the number one use of the Jefferson National Forest. There are 950 miles of hiking trails, including 300 miles of the Appalachian Trail. Another special trail is the 68-mile Virginia Highlands Horse Trail for horseback and wagon use. Eleven designated wilderness areas in the Jefferson National Forest total 47,872 acres and offer primitive off-road camping.

Wildlife found in the Jefferson include such wide-ranging animals as the whitetail deer, black bear and wild turkey, as well as less common, potentially threatened or endangered species such as the New England cottontail, longtail shrew, least weasel, Cooper's hawk, sharp-shinned hawk, orange-fin madtom, sharphead darter, green salamander and thunder ridge salamander.

WITHIN THE JEFFERSON NATIONAL FOREST

Mt. Rogers National Recreation Area—The 154,000-acre Mt. Rogers National Recreational Area lies west of the Blue Ridge Parkway near Trout Dale, Virginia. This mountainous area varies in height between 2,000 and 5,700 feet. At lower elevations oak-hickory forests dominate, while northern hardwoods like maple, birch and beech are found at mid-elevations, and red spruce grow on the highest summits. Round-leaf birch, one of the rarest tree species in North America and listed as an endangered species, grows here as well.

The higher southern end of the NRA, including Whitetop Mountain, Mt. Rogers and Pine Mountain, consists of resistant metamorphic rock of the Blue Ridge province, while the lower, northern section is composed of sedimentary rocks of the Valley and Ridge province. An auto road goes to the top of Whitetop Mountain—the highest point one can drive to in Virginia.

Wildlife in the NRA includes at least 55 species of amphibians and reptiles, 30 species of fish, 50 species of mammals, plus more than 160 species of birds. Of significance is the occurrence

GEORGE WUERTHNER

Above: *East of Jonesville in southwestern Virginia.*

Facing page: *Active by day, gray squirrels are likely to "scold" hikers who interrupt their food gathering.*

of 16 species of salamanders on the Mt. Rogers-Whitetop summit area alone.

Whitetop Laurel Gorge—The 800-acre Whitetop Laurel Gorge is between Damascus and Konnarock. A clear trout stream has cut a lovely steep-walled rock gorge. Within the dark recesses of this gorge grow scattered eastern hemlock, rhododendron, and cove hardwood species.

Little Laurel Creek—Old-growth northern hardwood and hemlock are found along Little Laurel Creek within the Mt. Rogers NRA. The creek is also home to a beaver colony. At the eastern end is Cherry Tree Camp, long known as an Indian encampment during the 17th century. Nearby Double Top and Round Top mountains offer beautiful vistas.

Little Wolf Creek—Numerous cascading waterfalls as well as a cliff-lined gorge are the main attractions of Little Wolf Creek. The Appalachian Trail corridor passes through the area.

Peters Mountain Wetland—Due to topographic features that block drainage, there are several wetlands atop Peters Mountain, which lies near the West Virginia border. These bogs support vegetation more commonly found farther north. Wildlife associated with the area include black bear, pileated woodpecker and wild turkey.

Hipes Branch—Hipes Branch lies in Botetourt County beneath Pine Mountain and Rich Patch Mountain. The stream itself is considered a good native trout fishery, and its sylvan setting among large, old-growth hemlock, birch and rhododendron makes this an excellent place for hiking and primitive camping.

Mountain Lake Wilderness—The only natural lake in western Virginia rests on a high plateau that now makes up the 10,753-acre Mountain Lake Wilderness. Located northwest of Blacksburg, this wilderness ranges in elevation from 2,200 to 4,100 feet. Attractions include virgin stands of spruce and hemlock as well as a segment of the Appalachian Trail.

Thunder Ridge Wilderness—Located along the Blue Ridge Parkway south of Buena Vista, the highest point in the 2,450-acre Thunder Ridge Wilderness is the 4,200-foot Apple Orchard Mountain. The Appalachian Trail runs through a portion of this wilderness.

Beartown Wilderness—A sphagnum bog and beaver ponds along with Roaring Fork Creek, a native trout stream, are among the attractions of the 6,375-acre Beartown Wilderness located northeast of Hungry Mother State Park. The terrain is rugged with few trails. The Appalachian Trail borders the southern portion of the wilderness.

Kimberling Creek Wilderness—North of Wytheville lies the 5,580-acre Kimberling Creek Wilderness. Hogback Mountain, at 3,200 feet, is the highest peak. Except for a few old, abandoned roads, there are no trails within the wilderness.

Lewis Fork Wilderness—The highest point in Virginia, 5,729-foot Mt. Rogers, lies within this wilderness. At these high elevations, spruce and fir forests more typical of northern regions dominate. With both the Appalachian Trail and Virginia Highlands Horse Trail, plus several other trails, it is not surprising that the Lewis Fork Wilderness is one of the most heavily visited wilderness areas in Virginia.

Little Wilson Wilderness—Immediately south of Grayson Highlands State Park and of the Crest Zone within the Mt. Rogers NRA, lie the 3,855 acres of the Little Wilson Creek Wilderness. The highest elevation, 4,857 Second Peak, has small stands of red spruce and Fraser fir, along with northern hardwoods like sugar maple, beech and yellow birch. Both Little and Big Wilson creeks contain trout.

Little Dry Run Wilderness—The only trail in this wilderness follows Little Dry Run, a native trout stream. The lack of trails may be why this 3,400-acre area along the eastern edge of the Mt. Rogers NRA is lightly used.

Barbours Creek Wilderness—The 3,800-foot summit of Potts Mountain is accessible by the only trail within this 5,700-acre wilderness. This remote area north of New Castle has forests of hemlock, white pine and hardwoods.

James River Face Wilderness—One of the first wilderness areas designated in Virginia, the James River Face Wilderness is bordered by its namesake, the James River. The area is well traversed by trails, including a segment of the Appalachian Trail.

Shawvers Run Wilderness—The 3,570-acre Shawvers Run Wilderness lies north of New Castle. Both Valley Branch and Shawvers Run contain native populations of brook trout, but the lack of trails means there is not much competition in angling for them.

Peters Mountain Wilderness—For fine views, the numerous sandstone ledges near the top of 3,956-foot Peters Mountain cannot be beat. This 3,326-acre wilderness located north of Pembroke offers a diversity of vegetation from upland bogs to oak and hickory forest. The Appalachian Trail and two other trails provide access.

Facing page: "The Towers" in Breaks Interstate Park on the Kentucky-Virginia border.

TOM TILL

FOR MORE INFORMATION

ROB & MELISSA SIMPSON

Fire pink.

Additional information can be obtained from the following sources.

ORGANIZATIONS

Appalachian Trail Conference
P.O. Box 807
Harpers Ferry, WV 25425

Blue Ridge Environmental Defense League
Box 1308
West Jefferson, NC 28694

Katúah Journal
Box 638
Leicester, NC 28748

Potomac Appalachian Trail Club
1718 N St. NW
Washington, DC 20036

Preserve Appalachian Wilderness (PAW)
R.R. 1, Box 530
North Stratford, NH 03590

The Nature Conservancy
1800 North Kent St.
Arlington, VA 22209

Western North Carolina Alliance
P.O. Box 18087
Asheville, NC 28814

The Wilderness Society
1400 Eye St.
Washington, DC 20005

The Wilderness Society
Southeast Regional Office
1819 Peachtree Rd. NE Suite 714
Atlanta, GA 30309

GOVERNMENT AGENCIES

Appalachian National Scenic Trail
National Park Service
Harpers Ferry Center
Harpers Ferry, WV 25425

Blue Ridge Parkway
P.O. Box 7606
Asheville, NC 28807

Chattahoochee National Forest
508 Oak St. NW
Gainesville, GA 30501

Cherokee National Forest
Box 2010
Cleveland, TN 37320

Cumberland Gap National Historic Park
Box 1848
Middlesboro, KY 40965

Great Smoky Mountains National Park
Gatlinburg, Tennessee 37738

Jefferson National Forest
210 Franklin Rd. SW
Roanoke, VA 24001

Monongahela National Forest
200 Sycamore St.
Elkins, WV 26241

Mount Rogers National Recreation Area
Route 1, Box 303
Marion, VA 24354

National Park Service
Southeast Regional Office
75 Spring St. SW
Atlanta, GA 30303

New River Gorge National River
Box 1189
Oak Hill, WV 25901

Pisgah-Nantahala National Forests
Box 2750
Asheville, NC 28802

Shenandoah National Park
Route 4, Box 348
Luray, VA 22835

Sumter National Forest
Box 2227
Columbia, SC 29202

U.S. Fish and Wildlife Service
100 Otis St.
Asheville, NC 28801

George Washington National Forest
P.O. Box 233
Harrisonburg, VA 22801